# Pressed Flower Pictures

### AND

## Citrus-Skin Decorations

# Pressed Flower Pictures

## AND

# Citrus-Skin Decorations

*by*

RUTH VOORHEES BOOKE

Photographs by Louis Buhle
Sketches by the Author

AVENEL BOOKS · NEW YORK

517112302

Copyright © MCMLXII by Ruth Voorhees Booke

This edition published by Avenel Books
a division of Crown Publishers, Inc.
by arrangement with D. Van Nostrand Co., Inc.

Manufactured in the United States of America
c  d  e  f  g  h

# Acknowledgments

This book should really be dedicated to the flowers whose bright faces have been my constant companions for so many years. But there are those of my own kind to whom I must also express my thanks and gratitude. For many courtesies over the years and during the creation of this book, I want to thank Dr. George S. Avery, Jr., Director, The Brooklyn Botanic Garden, and also the many members of the Garden staff who have been so helpful. To Miss Alix S. Cameron, my former teacher and very good friend who gave me the antique lampshade used as an illustration; to Mrs. Charles Doscher, assistant secretary, director, and chairman of the lecture committee of The Horticultural Society of New York, who has graciously allowed the use of the picture of the Flora's Chain that I had made for her; to Mrs. E. Enid Grote, librarian of the Horticultural Society, for her many years of helpful friendliness; to Mr. Richard B. Farnham, executive secretary of the Society, for his constant encouragement during my work with the Society's flower shows and in the development of my pressed-flower picture hobby; to Miss Mary

## ACKNOWLEDGMENTS

R. Mackey, executive secretary of the National Plant, Flower, and Fruit Guild, for much generously given assistance—to these my indebtedness is gratefully acknowledged.

To Helen Van Pelt Wilson, who perhaps first saw in my hobby the book you are now reading, I am most deeply appreciative. To Miss Dorothy M. Voorhees, whose continuing help and interest over many years far transcended her duties as a librarian. And to Mr. Robert W. Voorhees, for his sympathetic help in the preparation of the manuscript, again thanks. As a flower book without pictures is hard to conceive of, to Mr. Louis Buhle of the Brooklyn Botanic Garden, who has so painstakingly and patiently taken the photographic illustrations, both in black and white and color, I am indeed grateful.

And last though not least, to my husband Robert A. Booke who for so many years has courageously endured the vagaries of a committed enthusiast and hobbyist—only some of which he could have possibly enjoyed—I offer my humble thanks. And to my sons Ogden Voorhees Booke and Frank Robert Booke—the twins—who in the first place gave me the idea of making these pictures.

Ruth Voorhees Booke

Brooklyn, New York
September, 1961

# A Thousand Pictures Later

Three years ago I gave up counting. That is when I seriously began to think of preparing a brief account of the hobby that I had followed for so many years. It was in 1937 that I made my first floral prints of pressed plant material. The making of things from dried flowers is certainly not a new art, for our grandmothers made passe-partouts of flowers from their gardens or of those commemorating some special occasion. There are traveler's scrapbooks over a hundred years old that have dried leaves, flowers, and fern pasted in them along with notes about the towns and cities visited. In fact, a pastime of elegant Victorian ladies was the making of flower bouquets treated in various ways to preserve them. But it would seem that if the art of using pressed flowers dried for decoration is much older in Europe, as might well be supposed, the records of the art are lost—or perhaps they are safely immured in the archives of some museum only waiting for some patient researcher to discover them. Opening an old book to find a pressed leaf or flower is an experience rather commonly encountered even today.

A THOUSAND PICTURES LATER

That others are interested in what has long been my own hobby is indicated by the many letters I have received from all parts of the United States and Canada asking such questions as, "How can I keep good colors?", "How long must they dry?", "Do tell me how to preserve the flowers from my daughter's wedding?", "Why don't you write a book and tell us how to make pressed flower pictures?". Such questions often make me wonder just what has aroused the interest of the questioner. Was there a family tradition of the making of such pictures, or was it the quite practical concern of the thirteen-year-old from Indiana who wrote to ask for the method I use so that she might in turn demonstrate it to fellow members of the 4H Club.

My own hobby grew out of the fact that there always was a family garden and that for years pressed botanical specimens had accumulated, first made for the purpose of making blueprints and for keeping garden records. With a wealth of material on hand, the picture idea does not seem an unnatural next step. The first pictures were, as I see them now, rude—just a few garden specimens in simple little frames from Mr. Woolworth's red-and-gold store. Soon the composition was more carefully studied and the frame more costly.

Then the cellar was explored and antique frames that

had lain packed away for years came to light; to design in the manner of old floral prints seemed the obvious thing to do. It would be nice to say that each piece of work surpassed the last, but in fact there were times in that first thousand that I devoutly wished another hobby had been my choice. That is the way of a hobby, it requires work and patience and constant recovery from discouragement. But what pleasure and deep-seated satisfaction when you can say to yourself "Well done!". Don't feel badly, if you become a little smug about it; on occasion even that is good for the soul.

There is so much more to the making of these pictures than the techniques described in the chapters of this book. As we work our pictures, we learn that Nature has found endless means of making of the flora of this world an infinite delight to the eye and mind of man. For centuries flowers have been used for personal adornment, from the wreaths of ancient Greece and Rome to the lei of Polynesia. Artists in all the cultures of history have found, in the flowers of their time, models to depict in line and color. To the poets, flowers provide the richest source of imagery to express their feelings and emotions. There are charming legends about flowers in almost every language—a gentle comment on the all-too-human nature of man's virtues and frailties. The nations of the world have all through history chosen a flower as their symbol just as they have a flag; sometimes these floral symbols have been adopted by people to exemplify their loyalty and pride in their homeland; in other cases they are chosen by legislative action, as most of the state flowers of the United States have been. Their religious symbolism is world wide.

The language of flowers is not merely a poetic phrase, for the names of flowers have indeed become meaningful. In olden times the sending of the flower of the columbine meant, unhappily, a charge of "inconstancy" on the part of the recipient, while the petunia in a lover's nosegay said "you soothe me," or a withered white rose sadly said "I am in despair." The romantic charm of this custom was still familiar to your grandmothers and grandfathers.

*In Eastern lands they talk in flowers*
*And they tell in garland their loves and cares,*
*Each blossom that blooms in their garden bowers,*
*On its leaves a mystical language wears.*

This quatrain by an unknown writer refers to the floragraphy of the ancient Chinese, whose chronicles antedate the historic records of all other nations. They seem to have had a simple but complete mode of communicating ideas by means of floragraphic signs.

x

Whether the reader of this book confines his interest to the making of pressed flower pictures or, as I sincerely hope, has an enduring interest in all things pertaining to the world of flowers, the avocation—this is really what a hobby is, a second calling—of working with flowers is one that gives an immediate and lasting satisfaction. Thousands of men and women, young and old, bear witness to this fact. Be patient and be imaginative, for these are the greatest talents you can bring to the making of these pictures.

# Contents

# CONTENTS

xiv

CONTENTS

Pepper—The Problems of Storage—On the Subject
of Varnishes and Sprays

PART IV   PRACTICAL USES OF THE HOBBY

# List of Illustrations

## LIST OF ILLUSTRATIONS

LIST OF ILLUSTRATIONS

# *Part* I

SELECTION
PRESSING
MOUNTING

# 1. Gathering and Pressing Plant Material

The preservation of plant life is an art. There are many who feel that no photograph in black and white or in color, however lovely, can ever equal the interest and value of a real plant naturally and colorfully preserved. The botanist has been collecting material for many years for his herbarium or collection of specimens and much can be learned from his methods, which will be described shortly.

## Selection of Plants

The process of gathering, drying, and conditioning plant material begins when the first bud appears in spring and continues long after the first frost has seared the less hardy plants. Then the evergreens have much to offer. Small pieces of cedar, juniper, arborvitae, leucothoe, and even some species of euonymus may be pressed. But these are only a few of the evergreen possibilities. There are many more you may try, for regional plant

3

life often produces rewarding surprises. So by all means try them.

Grasses of all kinds, weeds, ferns, herbs, and foliage, as well as flowers, can be prepared for decoration under glass. Many of the fleshy flowers present special problems that require special treatment; but they too can be used.

The botanist will choose only the most perfect specimens for his herbarium, selecting carefully from fields and woodlands, the roadside and the garden. Both botanists and floral artists must take particular care of collected material in order to retain as much of the original color as possible. An efficient container in which to carry material is the vasculum, a small botanical specimen box, best when made of japanned tin; this box will keep most plants in good condition for a whole day, and it is indispensable in windy weather. Flowers picked for pressing are not to be placed in water, as you may surmise.

## When To Gather

The best time to gather plant material is in the middle of the day after the sun has dried out all of the surface moisture. In processing, it is more difficult to handle and preserve plants collected during humid weather. For those of us living near the seacoast and in the big river valleys it is frequently humid during the summer grow-

4

ILLUSTRATION 1

The Vasculum. The standard type used by botanists for collecting and
holding specimens until pressed.

ing season, so we must do the best we can and work quickly to start the processing as soon as possible after the specimens have been picked.

*Best Material To Use*

Select only the freshest and most nearly perfect plant material. All stages of development from the bud to the fully opened flower provide good material to work with. Reject any flowers past their prime. Plenty of foliage should be collected too and used with the flowers to add interest and variety to your floral designs. Flowers which are beginning to go to seed or have gone to seed and which show an arresting structure add interest and will give subtle variation in pictures. So do not neglect to pick them and use them.

Fleshy or thick-textured flowers such as the passion-flower, waterlily, or dahlia are not always easy to press, though success may be obtained if special care is taken in processing. Also difficult to press are the thin-textured flowers like the lilies, nasturtiums, petunias, poppies, hollyhocks, and others of similar petal texture. When they are dry their petals become most delicate and transparent and tissue-thin. Great care is required in handling them.

Flowers such as the larkspur, pansy, coxcomb, heather, helenium, zinnia, marigold, delphinium, black-eyed Susan, geranium, daisy, candytuft, bee balm, and a great many others will hold their natural color very well and are much easier to handle when fully dry because they have firm textural quality.

On the other hand the wisteria, violet, sweet pea, lily-of-the-valley, nicotiana, and a number of other flowers do not retain their color successfully. They rather uniformly turn to a cream or sepia color. Only pressing will disclose whether the less common flowers you may collect will hold or will lose their color.

Yellow or orange flowers rarely change color when dried. Larkspur and delphinium—all colors—remain unchanged. Only a few of the reds retain the original color: some darken a bit, while others will dry a little lighter. Pink flowers usually hold true to color, but the lavenders and purples frequently change. The blue hydrangea is a tricky flower to press; the blue blossoms keep their color most of the time, but on occasion the desired blue will turn either lavender or pink. The pink hydrangea sometimes holds its color, but then again it will dry lavender. The lavender form sometimes turns pink or blue. However, they are all pretty and can be used whatever the color.

Do not discard any of your pressed material because it has faded, for it may be used here and there among brightly colored blossoms or it may be grouped together on very bright backgrounds. Other uses for faded material are suggested in later chapters. Quite attractive is the sepia-colored arrangement placed on a bright-colored cloth or paper background. White flowers which have turned a cream color and others which are either a tan or brown look stunning on a dark brown chenille or dark green felt background when mounted in a gold frame.

It was not too long ago that I used lily-of-the-valley that had turned a soft creamy color, as it usually does, and arranged it on a brown chenille background. The delicate cream-colored flowers and the shaded tan leaves against the dark brown background looked truly lovely when placed in a frame of brown, lighter than the velvet yet darker than the leaves of the flowers. You will find as you work with dried plant material that almost all of it finds a place somewhere. So unless the pressings are mildewed they can frequently be used to good advantage in one or another of your pressed flower pictures or in some other flower craft.

---

ILLUSTRATION 2

Lily-of-the-valley, which rarely holds its color, makes a charming sepia print. Background, brown chenille; frame, walnut finish.

*Preparation for Pressing*

All of the specimens that you have collected for pressing must be arranged so as to appear exactly as you want them to when dried. Once they have dried, there can be no reshaping or rearranging of the pressed form. For this reason, bring to your first laying out of the material all the imagination at your command. If you can, try to visualize the way in which a pressed flower or leaf may be used in some picture you will later make. The graceful curve of a stem, a bent or folded leaf, the underside of a leaf or petal, an occasional stiffness for linear effect, full face or side view, these are some of the ways you can consider when you prepare your specimens. Sometimes it is easier to cut off the flower head from the stem and press each separately. The stem can be added to the flower later when you are designing your picture.

Sprays of foliage or flowers need to be pruned somewhat so that they do not have a bulky appearance, that is, the mass does not overwhelm the texture, the color, and the line of the specimen. So when pruning, cut or snip off surplus or unwanted leaves and florets—these are to be pressed separately—and then the material will not be too thick. In other words, do not have leaves and flowers on top of each other. This thinning-out procedure does the same thing for the pressings as it does for the gardener when he transplants seedlings to get better plant development. At first it will be better to be somewhat ruthless in your pruning rather than otherwise. For the beginner, trial and error will doubtless be the best teacher; certainly I found it so. The fleshy and thick-textured flowers handle more easily when placed face down on the drying paper.

## The Botanist's Method of Pressing

Rapid drying under suitable pressure is the key factor in securing good, permanent dried specimens of plant life. This factor is far too often overlooked and must be stressed both for those who follow the botanist's method and for those who use the simpler home method, as I do for most of my work.

Newsprint, used in both methods, is the paper stock used for the printing of our daily and weekly newspapers throughout the country. A word of caution: do not use newsprint that has been printed with inks other than the traditional black. The use of colored inks may well reduce the desired absorbency, for some of the color printing processes require a sizing to be put on the paper before printing. The botanist normally uses unprinted news-print for his work.

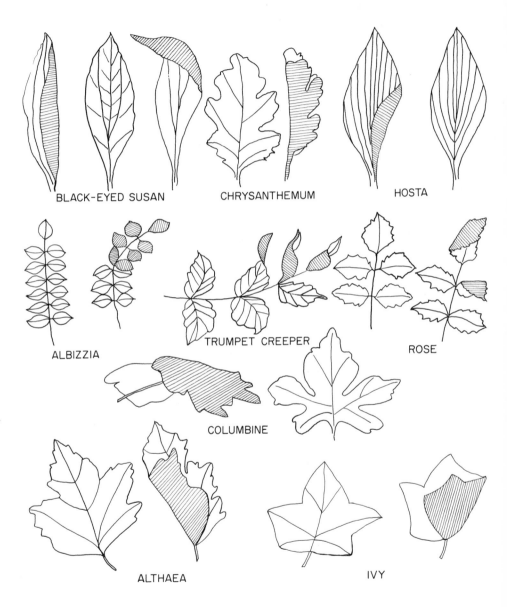

BLACK-EYED SUSAN    CHRYSANTHEMUM    HOSTA

ALBIZZIA    TRUMPET CREEPER    ROSE

COLUMBINE

ALTHAEA    IVY

Fig. 1  Leaves—bending for pressing

## GATHERING AND PRESSING PLANT MATERIAL

In the botanist's method, the folded newsprint sections, with the specimens of flower or foliage carefully positioned, are placed between two felt driers. These driers are of the same size as the folded sections used. For large quantities of plant specimens these driers are placed in stacks with corrugated pasteboard, which serves as a ventilator, between the driers. With a wooden-slat frame at the bottom, the stack is built up in this fashion: drier, specimen, drier, ventilator, drier, specimen, drier, ventilator, and so on. On the top of the completed stack another frame is placed and the entire bundle is then bound with two strong straps, such as trunk straps. A stack can be built up in this way as much as three feet in height. The straps are then tightened, though not too tightly as too much pressure may mash or bruise the softer or more delicate parts of the specimens.

To facilitate drying, the bundle is then exposed to the sun and wind. Or, if more practicable, it may be placed near a heating element such as a stove; however it should never be placed directly over a radiator of any kind. A gentle, steady flow of heat is what is required.

For plants that have been placed in the press in the morning the driers should be changed the same evening. A second change of the driers will be necessary the following day.

13

The great majority of the specimens will be perfectly dry in thirty-six to forty-eight hours after being put into the press. But, if a specimen feels moist to the palm of the hand, the drying process should be continued until all moisture has completely disappeared. When it is found that the specimens are perfectly dry, the newsprint sections containing them are removed from the stack and with careful handling are tied up in workable bundles, properly labeled; they are then stored flat until the material is to be used. This is the way the botanist presses his material and it is a good method.

*Simple Home Method*

Instead of using all the special equipment which the botanist will use for pressing, I have found it possible to make use of large magazines to hold the newsprint sections. Two plywood boards, cut to size, are used in place of the slatted frames to form the bottom and top of the stack or piles of assembled newsprint sections. Weights can be improvised from many things around the house— large and heavy books, bricks, old-fashioned sadirons (flatirons the Chinese laundryman still seems to use), anything that you can handle easily and quickly, with a fairly large undersurface that will "stay put."

Having tried all kinds of absorbent papers, I person-

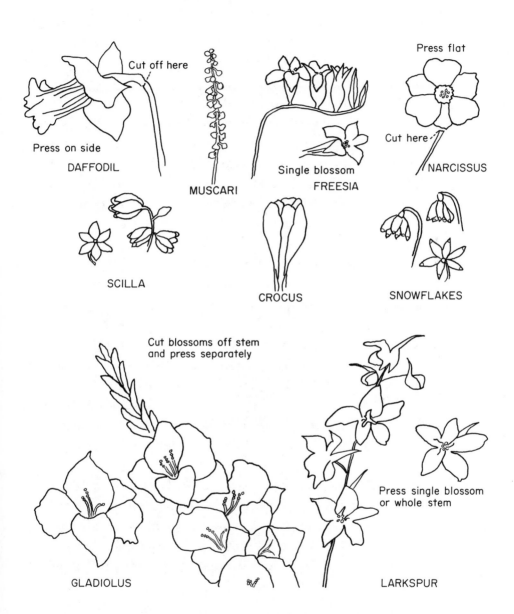

Fig. 2  Flowers—arrangement for pressing

ally prefer newsprint because I have found it most successful. It is barely possible that there is something in printers' ink that helps to preserve the color of the pressed plant material. In any case it's a nice thought. For preserving plant material at home there must be an ample supply of well-dried newspapers, old telephone books, or other kinds of absorbent papers, such as paper toweling or facial tissue, to use for the absorption of moisture from your plant materials.

If you prefer to use paper toweling, you will find that it is absorbent, to be sure, but when drying delicate flowers such as the cosmos or petunia, the slightly rough surface of the paper is likely to leave marks on the fragile petals. Certain types of paper napkins might do the same thing. Smooth and absorbent as facial tissues are, you are apt to find that delicate plant material will cling to them and will sometimes tear apart as it is being removed from the tissue. Certainly household papers with embossed surfaces or moisture resistant finishes of any kind will not be suitable.

The first step, then, is to have ready and at hand the working materials you will use—your freshly collected plant material, the papers, magazines, and other things— and ample clear space for working. The second step is to recall the points I have indicated above—on the subject

16

ILLUSTRATION 3

Fresh flowers are arranged on newsprint folders, with the stem and flower head pressed separately and no pieces touching. The daisy is placed face down to help keep the petals from curling, a technique recommended for specimens with thick calyxes.

of preparation of specimens for pressing—that are so important in the later use of your pressed flowers and foliage. Many ideas on pattern variation can be observed in the illustrations throughout the book. The third step is—

*The Placing and Pressing of Specimens*

Prepare folders made up of four thicknesses of newsprint and trim slightly less in size than the magazines you will use. These folders or sections will have four sheets above and four below the plant material when it has been placed in position and the folder closed. Set carefully aside and continue until you have made up as many of these folders as you wish to process.

You are now ready to place the newsprint folders in the magazines. Starting at the back of the magazine, gently insert the folders, with their artistically arranged specimens, seven or eight pages from the back cover. Leave several pages again and put in a second folder. Continue procedure until the magazine is filled. Don't use too many folders in any one magazine lest it become too bulky or bumpy and cause the material to press unevenly.

Now place the filled magazines on the bottom board, never stacking them more than twelve inches high, and then put on the top board. Weight the whole pile down

ILLUSTRATION 4

Newsprint folders are carefully closed and are placed in magazines; seven or eight pages are left at the ends and between the folders for the best over-all distribution of pressures.

with carefully adjusted weights, distributing the pressure as evenly as possible over the top board.

Until it is completely dry or dehydrated, all the plant material should be transferred very carefully into dry newsprint folders *every twelve hours*. The stack is again built up and weighted as before and the process continued as long as necessary. (The used folders can be dried out, stored, and reused as needed, except those that contain mildewed specimens, in which case the sheets are best discarded.) You cannot expect good results if you leave the specimens between damp drying papers. Dampness tends to turn most flowers brown, and you will find mildew quickly making its appearance.

*Drying Time*

In drying plant material it is hard to tell exactly how long before it will be perfectly dried out. If the weather is damp and humid, it will take longer than when materials are processed in dry sunny weather. Atmospheric conditions are indeed a ruling factor in this art. In a damp or rainy climate or processing period, artificial heat is usually required. Placing the stacks in metal boxes which are then heated by a 10-watt electric light bulb is an effective way of providing controlled warmth. But frequent checking is necessary to insure even heating if this device is

20

## ILLUSTRATION 5

The stack of magazines is placed between two plywood boards and weighted. Stacks a foot or so high are easiest to handle. Here flatirons have been used but other kinds of weights will do the job as well.

used. If artificial heat must be employed, you will try to approximate as closely as possible the steady, radiating warmth of a bright sunny day.

Another consideration that affects drying time is the type of material that you have used in your folders. If, for example, the material is fragile and delicate by nature, such as the alyssum, nasturtium, cosmos, petunia, buttercup, pansy, larkspur, and blossoms of similar texture, only a few days will be required before dehydration is complete. Larger flowers and those with thick-textured petals like the marigold and zinnia as well as those that have more than one row of petals will take from seven to ten days to dry. Should the texture be like that of the waterlily or passion flower, which normally contain much more moisture in their petals, it may take as much as two to three weeks for the drying period. The twelve-hour schedule for changing the drying papers, which is a must in the drying process, will also, as you can see, give you a regular check on the progress of the dehydration of your specimens.

*Storing the Pressed Material*

When the plant material has become dry, it is ready to be sorted and stored away in some safe, dry, cool place until it is needed for picture-making. First it is removed

from the newsprint folders and gently separated and or-
ganized. Don't worry if you have a pressed flower or two
that was perverse enough not to behave as you planned
it should. Experiment and experience are in this case not
costly teachers. Keep all similar material together, pref-
erably stored in manila folders, which are then labeled
and dated. Because this pressed material will keep and
last for years—and I have such quantities of it—I like to

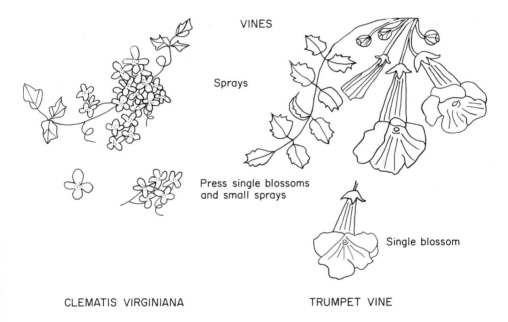

VINES

Sprays

Press single blossoms
and small sprays

Single blossom

CLEMATIS VIRGINIANA                TRUMPET VINE

Fig. 3   Vines—sprays and single flowers

know which is the newest. Therefore my own labeled folders are stored on shelves in a wooden cabinet with doors, one that is used just for this special hobby. They are filed alphabetically: acacia in one folder, ageratum in the next, bleeding heart in a third, and so on down the list.

A word of caution: It is necessary to place moth balls in the cabinet, boxes, or wherever the material is stored. The reason for this is that insects sometimes appear, apparently out of nowhere, and chew tiny holes in the flow-

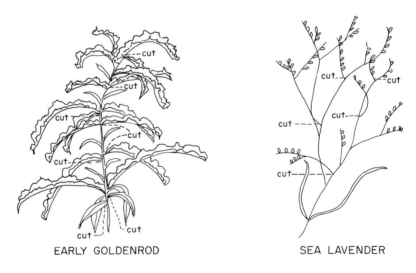

EARLY GOLDENROD                    SEA LAVENDER

Prune so that stems do not overlap

Fig. 4   Pruning—goldenrod and sea lavender

ers and foliage. Such imperfections make the specimens unusable for most purposes; the moth balls do nicely in preventing them. Always store your pressed plant material in as cool and dry a place as you can find until it is to be used. More pressed material was lost on the South Shore of Long Island, where we used to spend our summers, than in the city, where the atmosphere seems to be somewhat drier.

## Collecting while Traveling

The true hobbyist will find it easy to have the basic pressing materials always ready for use. Just remember to slip a few magazines and newspapers in the trunk of your car when you are going on a trip or taking a short ride. Whenever you spot some interesting plant life for your collection you can easily slip your find between improvised newsprint folders and into the pages of a magazine. Be sure that its picking is permitted, for it may be on the various state conservation lists, or the property may be posted against trespass and the picking of plantings. Always carry a weight of some kind to place on top of your collected material if you plan to be away from home for more than a few hours.

# 2. Frames and Backgrounds

Seldom in art galleries and museums will you find the paintings and etchings and prints displayed without a frame. Frames have the utilitarian function of protection, but they serve an artistic purpose as well, in that they delineate the limits of the picture against the wall or surface on which it is placed or hung. The frame enables the viewer to see the picture whole, as it were, without the distraction of whatever decorative qualities are present on the adjacent surface, and with which the art must otherwise compete. For pressed flower pictures, this aesthetic principle holds true but, additionally, framing under glass protects the fragile texture of the composition from movement, moisture, dust, and the effects of atmospheric change.

---

ILLUSTRATION 6

A carefree arrangement uses blue hydrangea as its focal point with lilac lunaria, lilac alyssum, yellow mimosa, and foliage of grasses, fern, columbine and mimosa leaves. Background: soft tan coarse-textured fabric; frame: maple.

*Selecting and Adapting the Frame to the Picture*

The frame and the picture background are more closely allied in flower pictures than in most framed artwork. In any case, you must keep an eye on both frame and background and be sure that they will complement each other. If you have handsome frames that you wish to use, then background and composition can be determined in their terms. On the other hand, if you have created a striking composition on a related background, then the framing should be chosen carefully to enhance the picture content. Flower pictures have definite color characteristics, and these too must be considered in choosing a suitable frame.

Quaint old oval frames, in old gold or in dark woods, around some dainty wild flowers and bits of grasses or fern or an arrangement in the form of an old-fashioned nosegay would be quite in keeping as period pieces. For modern pictures, plain painted or unpainted frames would give a posterlike effect when used with a bold design of

---

ILLUSTRATION 7

A mass arrangement using purple clematis, yellow gladiolus, freesia, and celosia, pink and rose geranium, white cleome, blue ageratum, purple alyssum, blue hydrangea, pink snapdragon and stock, and lavender hosta. Foliage is delphinium, ivy, and dusty miller leaves, with grasses and fern. Background: light tan grass cloth with decorated white mat; frame: white and gold.

large leaves and brightly colored flowers and placed where a strong decorative accent is wanted. Long panels, simply framed, are both interesting and effective when composed just of ferns or grasses or of leaves without the color complement of flowers.

Pictures in pairs are always a smart decorator's device. A set or series of five or six, framed exactly alike and placed step-fashion on the staircase wall, would look striking. A group of four small designs, say six by nine inches, is another idea that could be used for the milkweed or marsh grass animal designs mentioned in Chapter 4.

An inventory of the frames you have on hand, from old discarded pictures that have been long forgotten, will often prove a fruitful source for your first work. Many an attic will disgorge some wonderfully useful material. After refurbishing and reglazing, if necessary, at the local hardware store, you will find old frames do of themselves suggest to you just the right design to be used.

Good antique frames that you have stored away or that can be found in most second-hand shops—what doesn't go to the attic seems to end up in these shops—can be filled with flowers and ferns to represent old flower prints. Of course your frames can always be painted in different colors to match or contrast with your particular decor. Old-

ILLUSTRATION 8

A matching pair designed to look like old flower prints. Left: coral bell, white clematis, blue cornflower and delphinium, rose zinnia, pansy, marigold, purple scilla, blue hydrangea, purple hosta bud, with fern. Right: narcissus, white clematis, orange marigold, yellow freesia bud, lilac alyssum, rose heather, yellow annual chrysanthemum, lavender hosta, with dusty miller and fern. Background: natural grass cloth; frame: antique gold.

gold frames in the traditional oval shape are always prized. I have two such antique ones within which garden flowers and foliage on a fine grass-linen background have been designed to look like old prints, and they are always admired. The old hand-carved walnut or mahogany frames that were popular years ago are simply beautiful with pressed flowers under their glasses.

Although special-order (special-size) frames are usually expensive, you might find it helpful to visit the shop of a framemaker or the picture section of a department store just to observe the wide range of available styles in stock sizes. You will often get ideas that can be adapted to the pictures you are going to make.

*Making the Picture Background*

The texture and materials you may use for the backgrounds of pressed flower pictures are almost as varied as the pictures themselves. You may use white or colored papers as well as the Japanese rice papers. Then there are fabrics of all kinds—velvets, felts, silks, linens, organdy,

---

ILLUSTRATION 9

A line arrangement that follows the crescent pattern composed of blue and lavender hydrangea, pink sand heath (jointweed), yellow pansy and fern. Background: dark blue suede paper; frame: white and gold.

monk's cloth, and the denims—that will give stunning results.

In addition to paper and fabric, I have used such diverse things as a card covered completely with the parchment-like partitions of the pods of honesty, which you may know as St. Peter's penny or money plant. Their silvery, satiny surface gives a delightful effect; the partitions, by the way, must be glued to the card used for the mounting. Sheets of sterile absorbent cotton gives quite a different texture. Or you may want to try milkweed floss which has a lovely soft appearance. To produce an effect like that of needle point, either gros point or petit point depending on the effect desired, the backing card is wound round and round with worsted to become the perfect background for the "petal-point" pictures which are to be described in a later chapter.

When I select the white art papers, I often tint the center of the background with pastels to blend with the material I plan to use. Pastel colors can be had in both pencil and stick form and are easy to apply. The colors are softly blended with a loose cotton pad. Water colors from the children's paintbox can be employed to give a different background variation. With both these mediums work quickly and lightly and you will produce interesting grounds that will brighten your picture considerably.

34

Tinted backgrounds are particularly helpful in cases where you have not been altogether successful in obtaining good colors in your pressed material.

As the background, whether cloth or paper, is not glued or pasted to the backing cardboard but is simply laid on, as will be explained later, any firm, smooth-surfaced card can be used for backing. Whether specially purchased from an artist's supply house or taken from a suit box or even the back of a large calendar, the cardboard must be trimmed to the exact size of the background. Of course the thickness must be such that it is possible to fit the entire assembly of glass, plant material, background, and card into the back of the frame and allow for the permanent fastening. Experiments with various cards you may have on hand will quickly show you what will work.

## Mounting the Picture Background

With the picture glass as a guide—the frame to be used dictates the size of the glass—a card is cut to exact size. Then the background, if it is to be of paper, is cut the same size. But when fabric is used, the cloth is cut one and one-half to two inches wider on all four sides, using the card as a guide. Laying the cloth flat and smooth with the card in the center the trim is drawn over the ends and sides and fastened. This may be done with Scotch Tape or masking tape of suitable width, or an adhesive of some kind can be used. Inspect the cloth to be sure the warp and woof are four square, that is, the cloth is fastened to the backing card so that the threads are parallel to the sides and ends and it lies perfectly flat and smooth. Another way to fasten the heavier cloths is to sew the overlaps with a strong linen thread, using long basting stitches going from end to end and from side to side. Last but not least, inspect the corners of the working side to be sure they are smooth and even.

When your backgrounds are in place, you are ready to construct the designs.

# *Part* II
## DESIGNING THE PICTURES

# 3. Techniques—Design and Procedures

The end result of the work of any artist, or of any good artisan for that matter, is what the beholder sees or the listener hears. This is quite as true of flower pictures as it is for the more familiar forms which we designate as art, such as painting, music, poetry, architecture, and the many other ways in which man has expressed himself in his long history. Behind all the arts there is a working pattern, a set of rules that help the artist to express himself in terms that the beholder will appreciate and so to use the materials and tools of his art to attain that end. Art that uses dried forms from nature is unconventional in material, yet it too follows the same underlying principles as do any of the pictorial arts that use line and color and design. These important principles are summarized briefly in the following sections.

*Design*

Even though you may have no special training in art

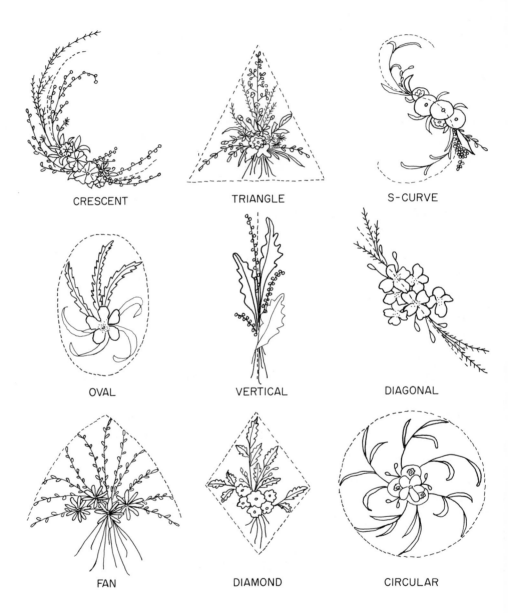

CRESCENT    TRIANGLE    S-CURVE

OVAL    VERTICAL    DIAGONAL

FAN    DIAMOND    CIRCULAR

Fig. 5   Forms of design—nine styles

techniques or in art history, you have all around you excellent illustrations that will help you. If you are a gardener, you will find them in the play of light and shade, of form and substance, of color and line in your garden. If smart clothes interest you, the way the designer makes use of materials, line, and decoration will be suggestive of the design principles employed. Just observe the flow of line of the modern household appliances you use daily. You will find design all around you.

In flower pictures, these are key "rules" to use:

PROPORTION—An arrangement that pleases the eye in its use of light and dark colors, of the relationship of vertical and horizontal lines, the spatial relationship of voids, or blank spaces, that are always different in size from solids, or filled spaces.

RHYTHM OR REPETITION—A simple motif that is repeated to form a larger whole. Nature, herself, makes use of this rule over and over again in the plant world. A good example of this is forsythia with its repetition of small yellow blossoms all along the branches. Larkspur and balsam show the same arrangement of small flowers growing close to the stem.

RADIATION—The arrangement of the parts of a design so that they flare or radiate from some central focal point or axis. The daisy and sunflower, as well as hundreds of

41

other flowers, show this pattern, with the petals growing in a whorl around the flower center. The placement of leaves along a stem in radiating fashion is common in nature as is the growth of stems and branches from a central axis or base.

BALANCE—The arrangement of a design as a whole so that it appears to the eye as a set unity in structure. In bisymmetric balance the opposing sides are alike or identical in design. In optical balance the component parts have the appearance of balancing each other, whereas they actually do not. This latter form of balance is frequently observed in trees growing alone in an open field or as a specimen in a formal garden.

*Four Divisions of Design*

There is a fourfold classification of design which is descriptive and identifying and is often used in characterizing the design. These are:

THE NATURAL—An arrangement within a given space that reflects the natural or realistic form of the subject matter without giving the impression of slavish or imitative copying. This is the concept that underlies most of the Japanese art forms.

THE CONVENTIONALIZED—An arrangement of the design pattern that utilizes the most typical lines and curves

42

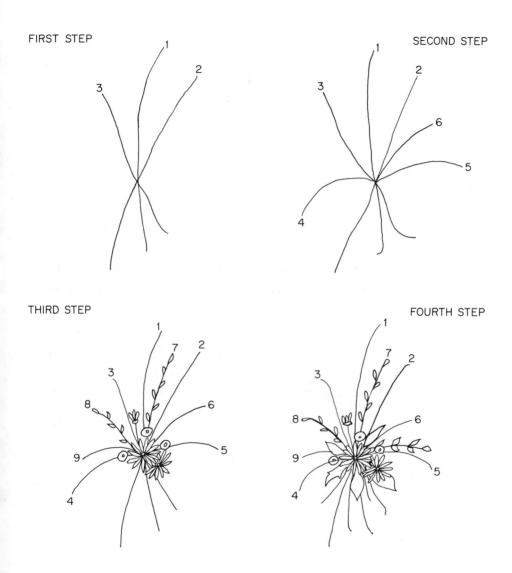

Fig. 6  Making a picture—four steps

of the subject matter and builds the design around these features. This form has a rather marked, observable pattern. Most of these designs are bisymmetrical or like-sided, though the optical or, as it is sometimes called, occult balance may be used.

THE GEOMETRIC—A design arrangement which strongly stresses geometric shapes and patterns with little apparent relationship to the natural form of the subject matter. The rhythm and radiation concepts are often used with effectiveness in this class.

THE ABSTRACT—A design that, while somewhat similar to the conventionalized, uses its material to the degree that it no longer reflects its original nature. Abstract designs are much used in all modern art and as such retain only the suggestion of the original; indeed, it is often hard to discern any relationship to an original at all!

In creating pressed flower pictures, the naturalistic and conventionalized designs are those that produce the best and most interesting results and for which the pressed material is best suited. Here are certain invaluable "rules" to observe in creating your picture design:

1. Avoid too many criss-cross lines and well-defined angles.

2. Do not use flowers all of the same size.

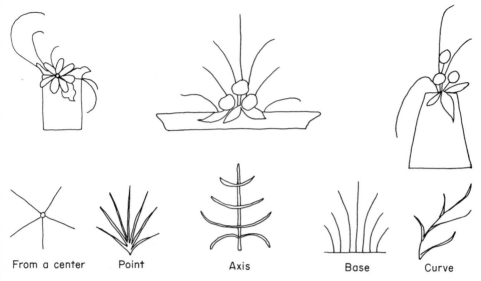

From a center    Point    Axis    Base    Curve

Fig. 7    Radiation

Fig. 8    Color wheel

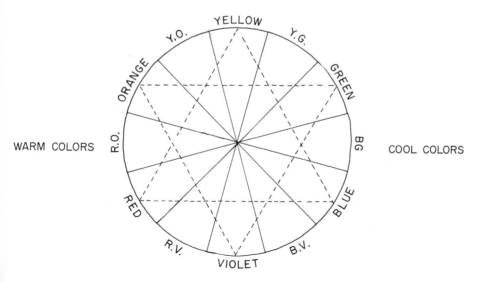

YELLOW
Y.O.    Y.G.
ORANGE    GREEN
R.O.    BG
WARM COLORS    COOL COLORS
RED    BLUE
R.V.    B.V.
VIOLET

DESIGNING THE PICTURES

3. Do not use too many different forms of either flower or leaf.

4. Avoid flowers that are too large or too small in relation to the design as a whole.

5. Relate your design to the frame that you will use.

*The Composition of the Picture Design*

The flowers have been carefully gathered and pressed and are ready to use. The frames and backgrounds chosen for the first pictures are laid out in orderly fashion. The four aspects—proportion, rhythm, radiation, and balance —are firmly in mind. Perhaps one of the many illustrations in this book has suggested the one you would like to make. Study this picture for a moment and you will see that it has what is called a structural skeleton.

This "skeleton," like that of the human body, is that on which the whole design is built. It underlies the three types of design used in these pictures: the line, the mass, and the naturalistic. Every composition of pressed material should have the basic elements of design. In both

ILLUSTRATION 10

A blue and yellow vertical arrangement. The yellows are the calendula, summer chrysanthemum, goldenrod, freesia and French marigold; the blue is larkspur; the foliage is grasses and columbine leaves. Background: pale green grass cloth; frame: walnut, with gold beading.

46

line and mass arrangements there must be a linear pattern. In naturalistic arrangements the plant material must be dried and arranged as it grows, a direct contrast to line and mass, where it can be turned and twisted to achieve the desired linear pattern. In essence the linear pattern is that which makes the picture "flow" and carries the eye from point to point without interruption, giving the feeling of continuity with each part well integrated into the whole design. The natural plant has this factor as an inherent part of its growth pattern.

If you want to, use pencil and paper to sketch out the varying forms of the linear effect seen in the illustrations. A rough drawing of your initial designs may prove helpful if you find it difficult at first to visualize the results. This will avoid unnecessary handling of your pressed material.

Added to the linear element there should be an interesting silhouette of well-spaced solids having between them nicely shaped voids and a good balance of visual weight of plant material on both sides of a vertical axis. This last may be slim, small blooms or buds or the sharp tips of slender leaves worked into the design along the outer edges at the top and sides.

The horizontal and vertical line and the mass designs may be either symmetrical or asymmetrical as you choose. When you are making a picture with a vertical axis, it is of course proportionally longer than the horizontal axis; the reverse is true when the design is horizontal. The words horizontal and vertical are used simply as directional in meaning and never in the sense of straight lines, for surely a design in which the material was placed in straight lines, either in respect to shape or texture or color, would be dull and uninteresting. Nature manages somehow to work graceful curves into all her growing things and so should we in using Nature's plants.

Mass arrangements also may have the quality of suggesting depth. To accomplish this, the material is placed so that flowers and foliage are close together and here and there overlap in building up the design. Some mass arrangements have a feeling of buxomness about them, while others using less material still give the effect of mass and solidity.

The illustrations show that the pictures may be made up all of flowers, all of foliage, or of both. Some pictures will stress the dominance of texture, others color or form or line.

Every picture that you will make will be an original, as you will find it impossible to duplicate all of your pressed plant material, so go ahead and sign and date them as all good artists do. To make it truly original, be original and imaginative in all your work and, if you don't have pa-

49

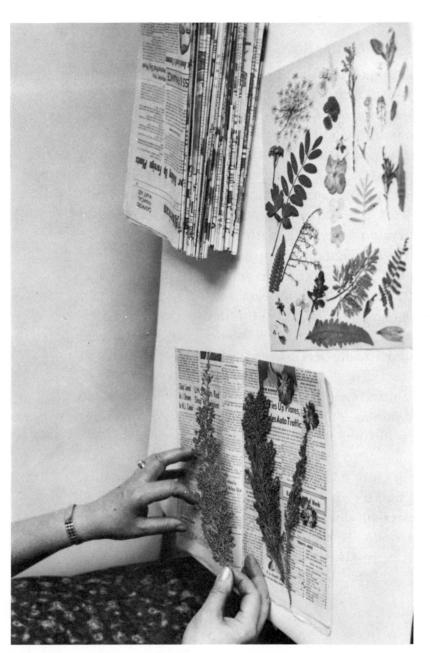

ILLUSTRATION 11

Dried pressed material is removed from newsprint folders and placed on cardboard sheets as soon as it is dry; in humid weather newsprint will reabsorb moisture and so is unsuitable for storage.

tience, begin right now to store up as big a supply as you can command for you will surely need it, as you may have already guessed.

## Making the Picture

First assemble the necessary equipment you will use; fortunately the list is not large.

Small tweezers — just in case you find your fingers not as adept as you thought.

Good-sized needles with fine points — to pick up and place the pressings on the background.

Good sharp scissors or shears with rather thin blades — to trim or prune away unwanted material on stems and sprays.

Needle and strong linen thread — to sew fabric on the backgrounds when necessary.

Transparent adhesive — in liquid form that dries transparent; Elmer's Glue-All or Sobo are what I use and reserve for use on very large pieces, as the trays or samplers, with very tiny bits of material; mucilage, glue, and cement darken as they dry.

Small pair of pliers — the kind silversmiths or milliners use; to handle nails in fixing the pictures in the frames.

51

## DESIGNING THE PICTURES

Fine wire nails or brads — practically headless; ⅜ and ½ inch for small frames, ¾ inch for larger ones.

Scotch Tape or masking tape — to fasten final backing sheet to the frame.

Secondly, have all the flowers, buds, grasses, foliage,

ILLUSTRATION 12

Pressed material is sorted and similar pieces are placed in labeled folders for future use. The folders are filed flat, not vertically.

ILLUSTRATION 13

Before a picture is started, all the pressed pieces, the frame and glass, the background, and the necessary hand tools are assembled. Tweezers are suggested for handling delicate pieces. The brush is useful for removing specks or broken-off fragments.

and other pieces that you think you will need and have selected from your pressed material folders, laid out on a large smooth piece of cardboard. Your selections of pressed material will of course be made in terms of the picture design you have chosen to make, one that you can see in your mind's eye. This visualization before starting work is a must, even though at first it may mean copying a design or following closely a sketch you may have made. Whether it is a pattern based on the form of the diamond, crescent, circle, oval, fan, triangle or the diagonal, vertical, or Hogarth line (a sweeping S curve, considered by its creator and by many as the most perfect line ever devised) your basic design will control the way in which you place your material, using form, line, texture, and color to obtain the best possible effect.

Thirdly—here is where your store of patience comes in —begin by placing carefully on the chosen background the first pieces of tall grasses, fern and sprays that will form the outer edges of the design; use leaves or branches of vines if that is your choice, perhaps a tiny cattail or young pussy willow shoot. This will give you a rough outline to be filled in. (Remember the pieces are simply laid in position, never fastened, for it is pressure of the glass that holds them in place.) Then continue to fill in with pieces that are varied in shape or color. Some of the pressings

54

may be tucked in part under another; some will overlay. Adjust as you add so that the voids and filled spaces give a pleasing balance. When you feel that the picture you are building up seems somewhat flat, add or change to pieces of more substance, or perhaps a more striking color accent will do the trick. When all the pieces that you want to use are in place, look again to your supply, just to see whether you overlooked one that might give you a more striking effect.

Now, study your layout a bit. Have you observed the five "rules" mentioned earlier under the Four Divisions of Design? Is there a focal point? Is it too high or too low? Have you used too much material for the frame to contain? Too little? It will be helpful at times to leave the work for a short time and then come back to it. This will help you avoid an overcritical viewpoint at the beginning. Often the slightest snipping here, careful pushing there, will be all that is needed to complete your design. Now view your picture from all four sides, for in this way an unhappy bit may be seen that might otherwise be overlooked.

The fourth and last step is to place the clean glass over the finished picture. So that not one piece in your layout will shift, this must be done with utmost care, by lowering the glass squarely over the background with its burden of

55

ILLUSTRATION 14

Glass is carefully placed over a completed design. Any shifting of material will necessitate re-doing the design.

your design. Then the frame is gently placed over the glass. Inspect to see if any shifting has taken place. This assembled unit—frame, glass, picture, and background—must now be turned over. To do this pull the unit toward you and over the table edge where it can be grasped by the hands with the thumbs on the sides of the frame and the fingers spread under the back with firm pressure, then turn over. The unit is then placed frameside down on the table and holding nails pushed in the four sides, firmly though not completely. Turn over and inspect for any shift of material. If there is any, well, you go back to the beginning! With a little practice you will find it less and less necessary to redo your work.

When you are sure that the picture is all right, gently push in nails all around the frame using the end of the pliers; space them fairly evenly. The number of nails will depend to a degree on the size of the frame and the thickness of the background card. Do not attempt to hammer in the nails, as this will more than likely cause some of the material to shift in the picture. A strong paper backing (wrapping paper does nicely) trimmed a little less in size than the frame, is then fastened on to seal out dust and moisture as well as to conceal the nails and background card. This paper may be secured by Scotch Tape, masking tape, or glue (not mucilage) to the wood of the

ILLUSTRATION 15

The frame is very gently fitted over the design under glass. If any shift-ing occurs, it will have to be corrected before the frame is turned over to nail.

## ILLUSTRATION 16

After the frame has been turned over, the nails are gently pushed in
all around the frame with the pliers—no hammers please—about three
quarters of an inch apart.

frame. Picture-framers use glue, but I find the tape does the job nicely.

An alternate method of lifting the unit is to slip a table knife or spatula under the side of the frame, using the fingers to lift and to hold in place before turning over. If the bevel at the back of the frame is fairly shallow, this trick works well. Have you forgotten to sign your piece? If you have, you might want to label your picture on the back with name, date, and possibly with the plant material used; a paste-on label will take care of these details.

# 4. *Adventures in Arrangement*

Perhaps by this time you have a good collection of pressed flower material collated and stored ready for use. Perhaps also you have tried your hand at making the more conventional designs and completed your trial-and-error experiments. The adventures that are to be found in this chapter presuppose a reasonable degree of skill and facility in handling the basic materials, for they are like the compositions that the pianist or singer tries after he has mastered the foundation scales.

## Petal-point Pictures

This name came to me suddenly one day while I was admiring a very lovely petit point chair seat. I thought to myself, why not make "petal-point" pictures? They would certainly be different from anything I had tried before.

Plain narrow frames seem best for this kind of picture so as not to distract the eye from the design. Then the background should reflect the pattern of the original.

First, cut a stiff, firm cardboard to the exact size of the glass and then at each corner of the card, an eighth of an inch from the sides, top and bottom, cut a V-shaped notch, one quarter of an inch deep. Choose a worsted or nylon yarn of a neutral background color and about the thickness used in petit point. Then tie a knot in the yarn three inches from the end and slip it into the notch at the upper left corner on the back side; or simply hold the three-inch end in place with your fingers or fasten it temporarily with masking tape. Now draw the yarn down to the notch at the bottom and around the card. Continue to wind round and round the card as you would a bobbin or as the weaver does in setting up the warp on a loom. Keep the yarn taut without stretching it and wind the strands very close together with lines straight. The winding is from back to front so that the last turn will end at the right bottom notch; then bring it diagonally across the back to the left and tie it with a double knot to the three-inch end.

Petal-point, as the name implies, uses the separate flower petals, so collect from your storage folders those that have separated in drying and such other flowers as you may need that can be separated. Tiny blossoms, single

---

ILLUSTRATION 17

A simple bouquet of wildflowers: field daisies, pink clover, yarrow, with various grasses and grains. Background: white water-color paper; frame: maple, with gold beading.

petals, and very small leaves are all that you need for creating the motifs to resemble needle point or embroidery.

If you have never made needle point, study a specimen to get the feel of its unique pattern and color blending. After deciding on your color scheme and your basic design, begin in the center of the motif and work around it by laying the petals, leaves, and blossoms directly on the yarn. The fragile material clings quite naturally to the yarn, but you may, if you wish, use minute amounts of Elmer's Glue-All to hold the tiny pieces in place. The standard method of mounting is followed after the design is complete.

As you can see, this work does take a great deal of time and an infinite amount of patience. Be original, for it is much more fun. But if you prefer to copy some design that you like, then do so by all means. Lovely border designs using petals and flowers can be made by this method, and even simple scenes are possible.

---

ILLUSTRATION 18

A "petal-point" picture, with petals and florets from white clematis, purple, pink, and white larkspur, Queen Anne's lace, pink and yellow celosia, lilac and white alyssum, and sea lavender; fern makes the greens. A blue hydrangea floret is in the center of the bottom unit.
Background: gray woolen yarn; frame: gold.

DESIGNING THE PICTURES

One of my own pictures has a light blue worsted background. The dainty border around the edge is made of lilac and white alyssum, fern, mimosa, and the smallest of all zinnias, yellow with a brown or purple center. The central motif is composed of many flowers: cornflowers, azaleas, violas, zinnias, larkspur, boneset, daisies, pink hawthorn, pink celosia, bits of goldenrod, and various leaves. It does, I think, resemble a piece of embroidery and is set in a narrow black eleven- by thirteen-inch frame. It was made in 1947.

*Copying Flower Arrangements*

With much care and a good store of patience, you can copy flower arrangements. When I heard Mrs. John R. Fisher lecture some years ago on her famous Williamsburg colonial bouquets and watched her demonstrations in making them, it inspired me to try and copy one as nearly as possible for a lasting picture. It so happened that I had in press most of the materials that she had used in one of

---

ILLUSTRATION 19

A full, mass arrangement is used to reproduce a Colonial Williamsburg dried bouquet made of garden flowers as described in the text. Background: gray-green silk pongee; frame: antique walnut and gold.

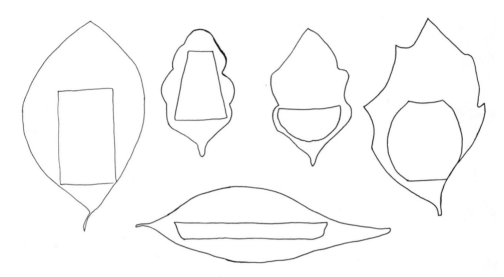

Fig. 9   Cutting containers from leaves

her arrangements. The problem was of course to suggest in two dimensions the rounded mass of the original.

I chose a lovely hand-carved antique frame, twelve by fourteen inches. The background is a pure silk pongee

---

ILLUSTRATION 20

A modern, vertical green and white arrangement, with three bamboo leaves providing the height. The white snakeroot flowers are set above snakeroot, coral lily, and rose leaves, seed-sprays of weed are at the left of the container, which is cut from large rose leaves. Background: white rayon cloth; frame: black and gold.

dyed a soft gray-green. Representing the original bronze container is a large pinkish-bronze leaf. Goldenrod, honesty, celosia, larkspur, calendula, Queen Anne's lace, sea lavender, pansy, fern, and grasses were used in this eighteenth-century arrangement made in 1948.

## Modern Arrangements

These too can be copied for both the line and the mass designs. A narrow strip cut from a large leaf might represent the base of a modern container. Another leaf can be trimmed in the shape of the container and fitted on the base. Then build up your design about twice the height of the container, with the material thinner at the top. You will want to have some of the leaves and blossoms falling over the represented container's edge, just as you would in a fresh flower arrangement. The design may be full or sparse, natural or sharply stylized. Except for the green container, a monochromatic scheme might be most effective against a complementary-colored background. Add a simple frame for a poster-like, very modern picture.

---

ILLUSTRATION 21

A modern, vertical arrangement that combines three pink albizzias and two pink gladioli with bamboo leaves. Background: water-color paper, tinted light pink and blue; frame: bamboo, painted gold and white.

## DESIGNING THE PICTURES

Refer to a text on art and color if you have forgotten the complementary color schemes or, better yet, get the always useful color chart or wheel at your artists' supply store.

### Coffee Tables and Trays

If you have become bored by the plain wood-under-glass of a tray or coffee table or tea wagon, try embellishing it with a design using pressed plant material carefully fastened with adhesive to the wood surface. A border design, a centered motif, or a simple line arrangement would look well. Should the wood be of good quality and finish and one you might some day want to return to, then simply place over it a mat or background covering of the desired color and texture and build your design on that. Adhesive is advisable here, for the constant handling and placing of objects on the glass creates uneven pressures that will cause the pieces of the design to shift.

Good-looking picture frames can be turned into trays. The same procedure is to be followed as for wall pictures. But an extra firm cardboard or piece of thin plywood

---

ILLUSTRATION 22

A contemporary arrangement using salvia in two shades of red with rough black-eyed Susan leaves. Four bottom leaves are bent to show top and undersurface, and to give a feeling of depth to the composition. Background: rice paper, tinted green with water color; frame: maple.

## DESIGNING THE PICTURES

covered with felt must be secured to the back of the frame to support the pressures of use. It is advisable to check the mitering of the corners of the frame to make certain it will hold; thin angle irons will strengthen doubtful corners. Using a background of gold, arrange bits of juniper, arborvitae, or cedar and red celosia in a circular design to form a wreath for a Christmas tray. Let your imagination go to work. And don't forget to use adhesive.

*Calendars*

How nice to send a gift of a calendar that you have designed and decorated with pressed flowers. Here is how you can do it. Early in the fall secure one or more of the small calendar pads—a single month on a page—that are available for the coming year. You have often seen them used on small advertising calendars sent out by local tradesmen, and they cost but a few cents.

Choose a frame of suitable size to contain the twelve months when they have been cut apart and neatly

---

ILLUSTRATION 23

A decorative calendar. Bamboo leaves define the two columns and months are held with adhesive left and right. Florets of coral bell decorate the year and the leaves. The central motif is a pink polyanthus rose with pale pink sand heath (jointweed) and purple alyssum.

74

trimmed and placed in an attractiv...
card stock or artist's smooth-surfaced...
the background the same size as th...
months in whatever pattern you h...
paste them down, being sure that they...
dar is printed on white paper then a...
suggests itself, or perhaps a sheet th...
with pastels would be interesting,...
white calendar sheets and the colore...
with which you decorate the layout. A...
produce exceptionally attractive resul...
unique. Of course the pressed flowers...
adhesive, lest they shift when the calen...

### Paperweights, Miniatures, and Pins

Around your house and in the shops...
perweights decorated with photograph...
Venetian spun glass, and so forth, so how...
pressed plant material? You have to pu...
weights, which come in rounds, square...
longs. Remove the backing and lay ove...
you are going to use. This may be leathe...
paper, felt, anything you have on hand tha...
including aluminum foil. Trim to the rig...
together firmly under pressure. Then g...

**1961**

**JANUARY**
S M T W T F S
1 2 3 4 5 6 7
8 9 10 11 12 13 14
15 16 17 18 19 20 21
22 23 24 25 26 27 28
29 30 31

**JULY**
S M T W T F S
1
2 3 4 5 6 7 8
9 10 11 12 13 14 15
16 17 18 19 20 21 22
23 24 25 26 27 28 29
30 31

**FEBRUARY**
S M T W T F S
1 2 3 4
5 6 7 8 9 10 11
12 13 14 15 16 17 18
19 20 21 22 23 24 25
26 27 28

**AUGUST**
S M T W T F S
1 2 3 4 5
6 7 8 9 10 11 12
13 14 15 16 17 18 19
20 21 22 23 24 25 26
27 28 29 30 31

**MARCH**
S M T W T F S
1 2 3 4
5 6 7 8 9 10 11
12 13 14 15 16 17 18
19 20 21 22 23 24 25
26 27 28 29 30 31

**SEPTEMBER**
S M T W T F S
1 2
3 4 5 6 7 8 9
10 11 12 13 14 15 16
17 18 19 20 21 22 23
24 25 26 27 28 29 30

**APRIL**
S M T W T F S
1
2 3 4 5 6 7 8
9 10 11 12 13 14 15
16 17 18 19 20 21 22
23 24 25 26 27 28 29
30

**OCTOBER**
S M T W T F S
1 2 3 4 5 6 7
8 9 10 11 12 13 14
15 16 17 18 19 20 21
22 23 24 25 26 27 28
29 30 31

**MAY**
S M T W T F S
1 2 3 4 5 6
7 8 9 10 11 12 13
14 15 16 17 18 19 20
21 22 23 24 25 26 27
28 29 30 31

**NOVEMBER**
S M T W T F S
1 2 3 4
5 6 7 8 9 10 11
12 13 14 15 16 17 18
19 20 21 22 23 24 25
26 27 28 29 30

**JUNE**
S M T W T F S
1 2 3
4 5 6 7 8 9 10
11 12 13 14 15 16 17
18 19 20 21 22 23 24
25 26 27 28 29 30

**DECEMBER**
S M T W T F S
1 2
3 4 5 6 7 8 9
10 11 12 13 14 15 16
17 18 19 20 21 22 23
24 25 26 27 28 29 30
31

trimmed and placed in an attractive layout on a sheet of card stock or artist's smooth-surfaced drawing stock. With the background the same size as the glass, arrange the months in whatever pattern you have decided on and paste them down, being sure that they lie flat. If the calendar is printed on white paper then a colored background suggests itself, or perhaps a sheet that is hand colored with pastels would be interesting, to complement the white calendar sheets and the colored pressed material with which you decorate the layout. A little ingenuity will produce exceptionally attractive results for a gift that is unique. Of course the pressed flowers are fastened with adhesive, lest they shift when the calendar is handled.

## Paperweights, Miniatures, and Pins

Around your house and in the shops you will find paperweights decorated with photographs, shells, beads, Venetian spun glass, and so forth, so how about some with pressed plant material? You have to purchase the plain weights, which come in rounds, squares, ovals, and oblongs. Remove the backing and lay over it the backing you are going to use. This may be leather, suede cloth or paper, felt, anything you have on hand that seems suitable, including aluminum foil. Trim to the right size and glue together firmly under pressure. Then go to work with

I. "PETAL-POINT" PICTURE

A design suggested by petit point embroidery, composed entirely of flower
petals and florets. Flowers and colors are described in detail in Chapter 4.
No adhesive was used.

II. SERVING TRAY

The florets and blossoms that make up the oval border include tiny maroon
chrysanthemums, white and lilac alyssum, pink and yellow celosia, sanvitalia,
browallia, blue and purple larkspur, ageratum, red bergamot, pearly everlasting, white clematis Virgin's Bower. The greens are ferns and small leaves.
Each piece was fastened with adhesive.

III. FLORA'S CHAIN

This original design, shown here in oval shape, was first made as a circle. Flowers and foliage are described in detail in Chapter 4. No adhesive was used.

IV.   THE PASSION-FLOWER (PASSIFLORA)
The flowers in this design are from the author's vines. The inspiring symbolic legend of the passion-flower is retold in Chapter 4. No adhesive was used.

## ILLUSTRATION 24

Paperweights, containing Johnny-jump-up, sand heath (jointweed),
wild oats, small pieces of coxcomb, and fern. Backgrounds: tan leather,
blue suede paper, white felt.

whatever design you want. Johnny-jump-up, alyssum, grasses and grains, larkspur, heather, sea lavender and other small flowers are excellent for this work. As the weights usually have a small space between glass and backing, you may build up your design a certain amount to give depth to your picture. An interesting design can be made of tiny cones, dried bayberries, evergreen tips, scarlet berries or barberry, and straw, all on an aluminum backing. When the design is completed and held in position with adhesive, fit the finished piece back into the weight—it must fit snugly—and finally cover with a soft, thin felt cut to size for a neat finish. Very narrow gold and silver paper lace strips, such as are used on decorated Christmas eggshells, will add an elegant and professional touch to your paperweights.

In place of flowers for someone who is ill, miniatures are nice. All the pressed material in these charming pieces is scaled down in size from the larger works to fit the frame, but the processing is the same. If a backing piece does not come with the frame, you can easily make one.

Pins are also novel things to make. You will need a tiny round frame with thick glass center, perhaps no more than two inches or less in diameter. All the pressed material you select will be the smallest that you have and the gayest. Proceed as with miniatures and back with felt.

ILLUSTRATION 25

A group of small (upper left) and miniature pictures. The largest is
actually five inches tall and the smallest, which is mounted as a pin,
is two inches in diameter. Miniature frames are usually metal, gold,
brass, or silver, and relatively thin so as not to detract from their small
contents. Backgrounds are best when light in tone and fine in texture.

## DESIGNING THE PICTURES

With Duco Household Cement or jeweler's cement, fasten a pin with a safety catch onto the back. In using Duco Cement, do not allow any of the cement to get on the dried plant material as it will remove all its color. Pins and paperweights are sold by handicraft stores and shops.

### A Poem or a Bit of Prose Illustrated

A handsome pressed flower setting for a poem or, as in my picture, a choice bit of prose, is most appropriate when the writing has some reference to flowers or the plant world. Such a piece is first carefully hand-lettered or written (in non-fading ink) in fine script on a sheet of quality paper or parchment—be sure you have a frame that will fit it, or have it specially framed if it is to be a favored gift. If you have a calligrapher friend, the results will be exceptionally attractive. Should your own handwriting have a characteristic uniformity, use it by all means. Center the poem so that it is in the optical center of the paper, slightly above center with the left, top, and right margins alike and a greater one at the bottom. An

ILLUSTRATION 26

An illustrated text. The tree is formed with pieces of cedar, placed against a scene of sky, hills, and meadowland done in water color. Frame: Victorian hand-carved walnut.

TO THE WAYFARER...

A Friend of Man the Tree Speaks

Ye who would pass by and raise your hand
against me, harken ere you harm me. I
am the heat of your hearth on the cold
winter nights; the friendly shade
screening you from the summer sun;
and my fruits are refreshing draughts
quenching your thirst as you journey
on. I am the beam that holds your
house, the board of your table,
the bed on which you lie, and the
timber that builds your boat. I am
the handle of your hoe, the door of
your homestead, the wood of your
cradle, and the shell of your coffin.
I am the gift of God and friend of
man. ye who pass by, listen to my
prayer.

HARM ME NOT.

off-center position can be used also, as I have done, if the weight of the decoration balances the text. Then, border the text with flowers and foliage, using those that are mentioned in the poem. As the surface of the paper will undoubtedly have a hard finish, it is wise to touch gently with adhesive each piece of material used and fasten it in place. Parchment has a faintly irregular surface which makes it difficult to prevent shifting even under pressure.

### Flora's Chain

In Roman mythology, Flora was the goddess of flowers and spring, and her festival, the *Floralia,* was celebrated in late April and early May. I have made a picture dedicated to the goddess which I have called "Flora's Chain." Possibly at her festival her statue was bedecked with such a floral crown or necklace. My picture, made in 1949, is composed of an oval of flowers against a white woven worsted background and is enclosed in a bamboo frame. I have also made a circular picture of Flora's Chain. The chain is made from the following flowers from three of the four seasons.

| | |
|---|---|
| aquilegia (pink) | calendula (yellow; cream) |
| black-eyed Susan | calliopsis (yellow; brown) |
| browallia | celosia (red; pink; yellow) |

82

cherry, flowering
chrysanthemum (pink)
clematis (Virgin's Bower)
cornflower (blue; pink;
   white)
cosmos (pink: Orange
   Flare)
daisy
gallardia (Indian Chief)
geranium (pink)
globe amaranth (pink;
   red)
goldenrod

helenium
hydrangea (pink; blue)
Joe-pye-weed
larkspur (pink; lavender)
marigold (Signet)
narcissus (yellow)
nicotiana (pink)
Queen Anne's lace
   (cream)
salvia (pink; red)
sea lavender
statice (violet)
zinnia (Navajo)

Foliage of various kinds is woven in and out of the flowers. In the parentheses are the colors of the flowers that were used; in a few cases the variety is named; the others were used in the single color of the flower.

## The Passion-flower

Few flowering plants are steeped as deeply in religious folklore as is the passion-flower. This tendril-climbing vine, a native of tropical America, was discovered in New Spain (Mexico) in the seventeenth century by Spanish monks following in the wake of conquest. Careful drawings of it were made along with those of other strange plants of the New World. Today about three hundred species of the passion-flower vine are recognized. Its English name is a translation from the Medieval Latin, *flos passionis*, of the monks who found and gave it its name.

The blossoms are very beautiful though odd in appearance—pink with a center crown of purple and white —and the Spanish monks, steeped in religious symbolism as they were, soon called it "the flower of the five wounds." Those sent as missionaries among the Indians of Peru regarded it as a divine sign to help in the conversion of the heathen Incas.

No flower has had so full a symbolic interpretation as the passion-flower. The ten petals represent the ten apostles who were present at the Crucifixion. The fringelike crown within the corolla was the crown of thorns, emblematic of a halo. The five stamens represented the five wounds or, as some saw them, the hammers that drove the three nails into His body as He was hung on the Cross.

---

ILLUSTRATION 27

A panel of leaves in shades of green. Dusty miller, snow-on-the-mountain, fern, pansy, coral bell, mimosa, columbine, ivy, delphinium, black-eyed Susan, cleome, and snakeroot were used. Background: white nylon yarn; frame: green and white.

84

DESIGNING THE PICTURES

The three nails were seen in the three styles with their stigmas. In religious lore, stigmas are the wounds of Christ that appear mysteriously on the bodies of others. No wonder that the beautiful flower had so strong an appeal to those who first beheld it!

For years I have grown the lovely passion vine, indoors in the winter in a sunny window and outdoors in the garden in summer. Sometimes it blooms in the house and it always blooms out of doors. The three flowers I have arranged in the picture (Color Plate IV) are from my own vine. The picture was created in 1955.

*Leaves, Just Leaves*

Leaves, just leaves alone are wonderful. Take any leaf and look at it closely. Turn it over and you will note at once that the two sides are not exactly alike. In color you will find the upper surface usually darker in tone and more glossy, as if it had been lightly polished. And the tints and shades of green are almost limitless, from the light yellow-greens to the darkest of blue-greens. In texture, the upper and lower sides are often markedly varied. Some are fine grained and show the rib structure, others have a pale, downy, protective undersurface; the thickened, sturdy character of the rhododendron and laurel or the succulents contrasts markedly with leaves that are

86

ILLUSTRATION 28

The bird in this picture is of marsh grass fastened with adhesive, the eye and beak, ink, and the feet, twigs. The perch is a speckled alder branch. Background: white water-color paper; frame: walnut.

fragile and easily wind-whipped into shreds. In Chapter 1 there is a drawing showing the variety of form in which leaves grow. Nature is indeed lavish in the minute variations she permits in the basic forms.

A panel under glass of leaves alone is so worth while. The different forms and shapes, the patterns of rib structure and veining, the infinite variety in color tones, all lead to the making of very rewarding monochromatic pictures. My panel in the illustration is of green leaves only. There are many plants that have colored leaves with reds, pinks, whites, and grays in light and dark tones. For some reason, probably atmospheric, holding color in leaves during pressing is much more uncertain than it is for flowers. The number of color cells and the effect of soil and altitude in various regions on foliage during the growing seasons may well be the deciding factor. (The parrot tulip is an example of color variation due to a disease of the bulb.) In any case, experimental pressing is about the only way to find out for a particular plant in your locality. Caladiums, I find, consistently fade, yet fall tree leaves hold true.

---

ILLUSTRATION 29

A bamboo panel, made with a hardy variety now grown in American gardens. The flowers at the bottom are a rose-colored rose-of-Sharon with blue scilla. Background: light gray poster board; frame: natural bamboo, ten by twenty-five inches.

## DESIGNING THE PICTURES

*Charming Animal Pictures*

Animal pictures sound like work for children, yet they can be delightfully and amusingly sophisticated. They are made from marsh grasses and from milkweed floss. The white rabbit is made by drawing the outline of the animal and then filling in with the downy floss. A lightly sketched background puts your rabbit at ease in his picture. Cats, dogs, and other animals of uncomplicated outline can be made in this manner. As you will see in the illustration, I have made a small bird perched on a branch of the speckled alder. How charming several of such small birds perched warily on a pussywillow spray could be!

# 5. Memory Pictures

The memory picture is one that recalls with pleasant nostalgia an event in our lives which in some way is both important to us and connected with flowers. The two do not often conspire together, but in the examples pictured and recounted here you may find suggestions for others that you will want to memoralize in this way.

*If a Picture Could Tell a Story*

In 1950, The Horticultural Society of New York celebrated its Golden Anniversary. As a tribute to the Society a picture of pressed flowers was made in tints and shades of yellow with green foliage and lettered in the yellow of chrysanthemum petals.

This picture was on display at The International Flower Show of that year and on being returned to its permanent home suffered an accident in transit that shattered its glass but without other damage. Later, with a new glass in place it was displayed and again some gremlin was on hand with mischievous intent. With necessary repairs and some nine years later it was shown, mounted

91

ILLUSTRATION 30

A memory anniversary picture. The description and history of this picture is given in detail in Chapter 5. Background: black felt; frame, gold, thirty by sixteen inches.

on a pillar. The plaster gave way, the picture crashed, and not only the frame and glass suffered, but the mounted pressed flowers went, as a sailor would euphemistically say, that a'way. Major repairs were made, following the original design, this time to bring it back to its first estate. The original yellow Giant Swiss pansies now show a purple throat, three double buttercups have become two, and some of the faded materials have been replaced, for the picture had been displayed for some time in a bright and sunny window. Other than this, the design shown in the photograph is as originally planned.

In this picture, as a kind of symbolism, there are representatives of the trees and shrubs, the herbs and vines, the grasses and wildflowers, annuals and perennials, bulbs and seeds. For the trees, there are speckled alder catkins; forsythia for the shrubs; and marigold and bergamot leaves for herbs. Thunbergia and the passion vine and wild oats and several kinds of grasses in turn stand for their groups. Black-eyed Susans represent the wildflowers as a native American plant. Among the annuals are the zinnia, coxcomb, celosia, sunflower, and summer chrysanthemum, while goldenrod, helenium, and the hardy chrysanthemum and others represent the perennial. The bulbs are typified by the narcissus and freesia and the seeds do service for all.

DESIGNING THE PICTURES

The four seasons of the year have their representatives too: spring with the forsythia, narcissus, pansy, buttercup, and catkin; summer with the rose, passion-flower, black-eyed Susan, zinnia, marigold, and helenium; fall with the single and double chrysanthemum, celosia, and golden-rod; and last, winter is symbolized by a bit of cedar with its tiny cones attached.

Then too the colors have their say. The yellows suggest wisdom, orange as the color of the flame in lamp and torch gives us their symbolic meaning of knowledge, and the greens bring to mind springtime, fertility and abundance.

In this anniversary picture, the narcissus and freesia were first used in an arrangement class of the Federated Garden Clubs of New York State in March of 1948. The Giant Swiss pansies were used at the Society's monthly show in February, 1949. And from an arrangement made as a tribute to the Golden Anniversary celebration in January, 1950, come the yellow rose and daffodil. Saved and pressed for the special occasion, they add a feeling of gracious sentiment to the memory picture. The flowers other than these special few, were grown in my garden, including the passion-flower whose story is told in an earlier chapter. Lest one wonder why this colorful flower was used in a yellow arrangement, I must confess that this is one of the cases where in pressing the flower lost its color and the resulting creamy tints fitted aptly into my design.

The four-leaf clover in the lower center of the picture is of course the traditional sign for good luck. The lettering is made from the yellow petals of one of the large "football" chrysanthemums, cut and trimmed to usable size; those of the giant zinnia were used in the original design. A last note on this picture must point out that because of its large size and addiction to travel, the dried material is fastened into place with adhesive, the triumph no doubt of virtue over valor!

## The Gardener's Heritage

I can not forego quoting here for you "The Gardener's Heritage", written many years ago by Liberty Hyde Bailey and America's great horticultural encyclopedist. It reads with a feeling of scriptural sincerity that sets it apart as a great botanist's epitome of life.

*The earth brought forth grass, herb yielding seed after its kind, and tree bearing fruit, and it was the third day. Thus was the earth prepared for man and thus to this day does man enjoy his heritage. To us it is the latest day. Millions of folks will come after us in other days. Yet their*

95

*days will be as new as ours, and not worn out. The grass will be as green and as eager as ours. May will shout for joy of new growths. July will nurture our crops and trees, September will produce the seed after its kind. Century will follow century. Fragrant lives of men and women will be lived like poems. As we in our golden age, plant the seed, experience the unfolding of leaf and flower, feel the confident hope of harvest, so will they in their time be born again with every new day. As centuries pass men and women will care less merely for gaudy creations of the hybridizer and will wish to live more closely with plants as nature made them.*

Surely Dr. Bailey is telling us that the memory of things past is never to be forgotten. Perhaps he is reminding us that the lowly buttercup is in the view of many botanists the Eve of all flowers and the ancestress to which all flowers have been traced on the Family Tree of Flowers. Or again, he may be warning us that the changes created by environment are common to mankind and the world of plant life alike, and that we should beware lest we forget

---

ILLUSTRATION 31

A bridal bouquet all in white flowers with fern. The flowers are larkspur and baby's breath. Background: white satin with lace panel; frame: gold.

our own heritage too. Will the gaudy creations of the hybridizer become symbolic of man in space? Just something to think about. For the time being, however, we still have weddings and their memories.

*Bridal Bouquets*

That brides never forget the details of the wedding and that grooms forget them forthwith seems to be a fact! Enough of a one at least to suggest that a memory picture made of the flowers of the traditional bouquet makes a charming anniversary gift.

For the background, a piece of the bridal gown could be used. A frill of net or tulle or lace from the gown could appropriately surround a tiny nosegay composed of a few flowers, buds, and greens. Streamers of narrow ribbon with tiny flowers might be used hanging in graceful curves. The bouquet itself will determine the nature of your design, as the modern ones contain such a variety of flowers. You may even find it necessary to employ the

---

ILLUSTRATION 32

A memory wedding picture. A picture of this type would, for reasons of sentiment, use flowers that were actually worn or carried. This design is made from white larkspur, blue delphinium, white baby's breath, pink roses, and fern. Background: white satin overlaid with pale pink and blue net on the left; frame: gold.

petal-point technique on occasion. Don't forget to work in the groom's boutonniere if it is available.

Similar pictures of the attendants' flowers can be made either separately or combined in one. White satin can form the background, along with small strips of the material used for the attendants' costumes; combine their flowers with those from the bride's bouquet. Here's the chance to be original and use your own ideas.

For these memory pictures, arrangement must be made in advance, so that the flowers and pieces of the bridal dress are available for pressing. As most such bouquets are made up by florists, the flowers will contain plenty of artificial moisture, so as much of it as possible must be removed before pressing. You might have to wait for several hours before processing. You will probably want to experiment with florists' cut flowers if you have not already done so.

Frames for these pictures seem most effective when white, silver, or gold is used; the size is of your choosing, but it should not be too large.

# 6. The Sampler with Pressed Flowers

The history of a word often reflects the story of an art. So it is with the sampler. In Middle English, that is the period of our language roughly from 1150 to 1500, the word *samplere* with the meaning of a worked piece of embroidery is first recorded in extant documents in the year 1503. The word came to English from the Old French *essamplaire*, and this in turn goes back to its Latin ancestor, *examplar*.

## The Needlework Sampler

The sampler as it was first known was a piece of linen or canvas on which were sewn examples of the various stitches employed in the making of clothes and in embroidery. It was made to preserve the patterns used and to serve as models for young ladies to follow, as it was quaintly described in a document of 1528. Soon it meant "a pattern of work, an example" and then an exercise in the art of stitchery using the letters of the alphabet, with

101

appropriate mottos and even verses, all in charming colors. These samplers were made by the young ladies of the upper classes to exhibit their skill in the finer arts of housewifery. Our penchant for all-inclusive terms gave us the word samplery for this art.

It was in 1502 in the account book of Elizabeth of York that an entry for July 10th tells us that the Lady Elizabeth paid 8d. (the "d" stands for the Roman *denarius* which has been used from earliest times as an abbreviation for the Anglo-Saxon or Old English word penny as the two were at that time of the same value; 8 pence is still today shortened to 8d.) for an ell of linen cloth for the making of a sampler.

At the Essex Institute at Salem in Massachusetts, there is a sampler worked by Anne Gower, wife of the colony's Governor Winthrop. The classical influence was still strong in those days for the W of her name is written as a V; perhaps the model sampler had no W, as this letter does not occur in the Latin alphabet and Latin in that day was still the language of the educated and highborn. This linen sampler of exquisite drawn work, with its linen-colored lettering, is the earliest authentic example of the sampler and undoubtedly crossed the Atlantic with Mistress Anne in 1628. Sampler art by then was popular throughout England and Western European countries, as decoration by means of hand-embroidery had been universally used from the fourteenth century on.

A legend has it that the needle and thimble were expressly invented for the making of the sampler. Sadly for the validity of this legend, it must be stated that the words both have traceable ancestors in Anglo-Saxon words, that is, prior to the twelfth century.

The earliest American sampler that has come down to us is the work of Myles Standish's daughter, Leora, made during the early days of the Massachusetts Bay Colony. Other notable specimens were made by Mary Wiggin in 1797; by Sarah Rush Meredith, sister of the famous Dr. Benjamin Rush who signed the Declaration of Independence, dated 1818; by Eliza Ann Perkins, aged eleven, whose sampler is dated 1829, and whose family founded the famous Perkins Institute for the Blind in Boston. All these last examples are in the famous Whitman Collection in Philadelphia. There must be many other samplers kept as heirlooms by American families; not all of them may be works of art in the usual sense, but they are treasured for reasons of sentiment. The period from 1790 to 1840 was the high point of the American sampler. During these times, the most elaborate designs and most beautifully stitched examples were made.

In looking for new ways in which to use pressed flowers, I thought of the sampler, and as far as I can find out the one I made in 1949 is the first of its kind.

*The Pressed Flower Sampler*

Having seen pictures of many beautiful and intricately worked samplers, and recalling the simple cross-stitch one of not too long ago, I could easily plan my design. A linen background, flowers from the garden and from the field, a border around the text, are its elements. From John Keats' *Endymion*, I chose the famous line, "A thing of beauty is a joy forever."

The border is composed of blossom petals and florets of

| | |
|---|---|
| larkspur (pink and lavender) | Queen Anne's lace |
| mimosa | celosia (pink) |
| bergamot | goldenrod |
| clematis (Virgin's Bower) | sanvitalia |
| creeping ranunculus | Johnny-jump-up |

and the foliage includes four kinds of fern, cedar, and sanvitalia.

The lettering of the quotation is made of rose-colored zinnia petals, mimosa foliage, and wild sweet pea (*tephrosia virginiana*).

The date is made of the buds of the wild sweet pea.

104

The floral unit at the bottom is composed of muscari, larkspur, and two kinds of fern.

And adhesive was required to hold all the tiny pieces in place.

Color Plate VI reproduces the effect of this design, made in 1949, and suggests the many possibilities that the floral sampler has. The greatest difficulty will be found in the reproduction of words with plant material. For your picture in this genre, do not attempt to reproduce the extremely fine lettering seen in many of the finest examples of the embroidered sampler. Better a beautiful seeming likeness, than an unsuccessful copy.

# 7. Botanical Studies

The difference between botanical studies and those pictures explored earlier lies in the choice of material and the simplicity of the design and also in the media employed—for blueprints, spatter prints, and ink prints. These studies are based on the design that Nature itself has created; sometimes it is a study of how the plant and flower actually grows; again it may stress the botanical structure of a plant or flower; or it may have as a theme the outline or texture of a plant. Techniques are somewhat different too.

*The Botany Prints*

Using the methods already described for pressing and mounting, you can make botany prints that have an un-

---

ILLUSTRATION 33

A botany print using lunaria. At left, a sprig showing natural growth, leaf, stem, bud flower, and seed head; at right, the development of the seed process with naturally dried capsule at the bottom; adhesive used for all parts. Colors: greens, lilac, pearly gray. Background: white watercolor paper, tinted with green and purple pastels; frame: bleached wood.

usual charm of their own. A series of such prints—they really should be called studies, for that is what they are —makes a handsome and distinctive wall decoration. Patterned after color plates found in early herbals and the older books on botany and constantly used as an illustrative device ever since, these pictures present the plant or flower as seen by a student of botany, a kind of artistic dissection. A single plant or flower is shown so as to illustrate the manner of its growth including its root structure, stems and foliation, bud and flower and seeding processes. All of these factors or only a few may be used to make delightful stylized pictures.

A zinnia print that I have made is framed in red mahogany and its background is a rough white cotton. A branch of the plant shows the graceful curve of the stem topped by the red flower. Several leaves are bent, to show both sides. Another flower is cut in half showing the underside of the petals. A section with the petals pulled off shows the calyx encompassing the seed-producing part of the flower. Another cut specimen shows how the seeds are fastened in place. At one side of the picture the seed is shown attached to the petal in various stages of development, observed from both the inner and outer sides. At the bottom, seeds are placed to show both sides. The

### V.  ANNIVERSARY PICTURE

This picture, commemorating an anniversary, features blue and white delphinium, feverfew, liatris, pink gladiolus, and the red rose; the foliage is rose and delphinium leaves and fern. No adhesive was used.

VI.   FLORAL SAMPLER

A design inspired by the art of sampler embroidery. The flowers and foliage are described in detail in Chapter 6. Each blossom, petal, and leaf was fastened with adhesive.

VII.   BOTANY PRINT

A design derived from the plates of sixteenth-century herbals. Old prints are always in demand for decoration today. Only the seeds and tiny pieces are fastened with adhesive. A description is in Chapter 7.

VIII.  EIGHTEENTH-CENTURY DESIGN

Larch forms the central line of this classic design. The butterfly is typical of the period. The flowers are lavender loose strife, coral bell, rose spirea (astilbe), scilla, purple and salmon salvia, pink polyanthus, pink nicotiana, hawthorn, blue hydrangea, blue larkspur, and lavender hosta buds. The foliage is columbine and ferns. No adhesive was used.

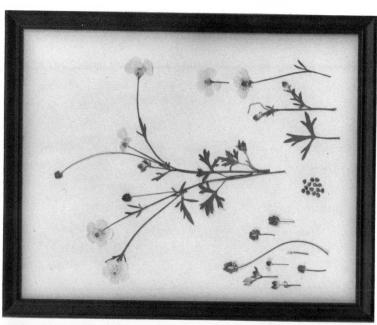

ILLUSTRATION 34

A pair of botany prints. Left: French marigold, dwarf single, var. Flash, yellow and mahogany flower. Right: buttercup, *Ranunculus fascicularis*, yellow. Various stages of development are shown. Background: white water-color paper; frame: black.

units are laid out in a balanced pattern to make an effective picture.

Such a picture-story can be made for all parts of a plant to indicate its characteristic growth pattern. Wildflowers that are not on conservation lists make stunning studies. Among those of special interest are the black-eyed Susan, the field daisy, and the milkweed. Goldenrod is good too when shown in various stages of development. The fern with its strong leaf pattern is another worthwhile subject to use. There is really no limit to the variety of such studies that can be made. Whatever pleases you will make an interesting picture.

A very simple composition of a few sprays of acacia or of evergreens with tiny cones, or one of buttercups and dainty grasses, for example, are all decorative, though they are not really botany studies. For such pictures choose lighter backgrounds for the darker specimens. The bright yellow of the buttercup is striking against a dark blue or black ground.

---

ILLUSTRATION 35

A botany print using the sensitive fern *(Onoclea sensibilis)*. Various stages of development are shown: creeping rhizome, young fronds, large leaf, and, on the left, the long-stalked seed panicle and seeds. Background: white water-color paper; frame: natural wood, with red beading.

ILLUSTRATION 36

A group of flower blueprints. Left to right from top: Snapdragon,
French marigold, butterfly-bush, cactus dahlia, celosia, cosmos.

## The Blueprints

The blueprint relies on the outline of a specimen for its decorative effect. It is a silhouette in white on a dark background and is an excellent way to use discolored or faded pressed material with an outline that is identifiable at first glance. The simpler forms do best in this medium but occasionally a sharply defined piece of more elaborate structure will be found that is suitable and effective pictorially. Single flowers or leaves as well as combinations may be used.

The supplies you need are simple: a picture frame with glass, newsprint cut the size of the glass, potassium bichromate, daylight blueprint paper, a darkened room, sunlight, and your specimens. Any small frame which has a fairly deep bevel at the back may be used: eight by ten inches is a good size. If you have a photographer in the family with a photographic printing frame, so much the better, as they are excellent for small prints. Daylight blueprint paper may be secured from many department stores as well as from handicraft shops or houses handling artist's and draftsman's supplies.

Using your darkroom or a room carefully darkened from outside light and with a red light to work by, the procedure is as follows:

DESIGNING THE PICTURES

1. Place the pressed specimen on the glass in the frame which has its bevel facing you.

2. Lay the blueprint paper, cut to size and with the tinted surface down, into the frame and over the specimen. Pack in newsprint sheets as padding very tightly so that the backing, when in place, will exert pressure. As the thickness of the specimens will vary so will the amount of padding needed to prevent light from getting under the specimen in any way, that is, between it and the blueprint paper.

3. Clamp in the backing and then expose to sunlight for about sixty seconds. Longer exposure will bring out more detail. Variation in the tone of the print may be obtained by underexposing for paler tints and overexposing for the deeper shades of blue.

4. Remove the backing, padding, and blueprint and immediately immerse the last in the prepared chemical bath. This solution is made of two heaping tablespoonfuls of the potassium bichromate to two gallons of water, measured carefully. Immersion time to be not less than five minutes.

5. Remove blueprint from the bath and wash in clear water. Then dry between newsprint sheets using slight pressure and changing papers several times to remove excess water.

6. Dry the blueprint overnight between dry newsprint.

These prints can be used to make many interesting things. Tallycards for bridge clubs, bookmarks, personal greeting cards, and garden records are some of the ways the blueprint can be used. Placecards with the names written in white ink is another idea. Decorative menus for that special luncheon will provide a provocative conversation piece.

## The Spatter Prints

A simple process, spatter printing is another way to use faded yet usable pressed material. A record of leaves in outline can be made in this way that will outlast dried leaves. It provides a novel way of ornamenting your stationery. And of course whatever can be made as a blueprint can be made in the spatter print.

What you need for this work is simple: clean ink papers (ink paper is that which has a sufficiently hard surface so that the ink rests on the surface and does not penetrate the body); waterproof ink, in black or colors, with white for use on colored papers; tempera or show-card colors, to be water-thinned; toothbrush or fine comb; small square of copper screening.

The first step is to lay the pressed material on the paper and fasten in place with tiny weights or fine-pointed straight pins so that it lies flat against the paper. Then with an inked brush, or use thinned show card color if you wish, in one hand and a small stick—a tongue depressor will do nicely—in the other, hold the brush over the paper and draw the stick upwards over the bristles of the brush using enough pressure to flex them slightly. As there are many variables involved, thickness of ink or paint, stiffness of bristles, and so forth, a little practice to obtain the right distance from the paper and the proper angle to hold the brush is advisable in order to secure the right intensity of the spray. The spray is carried around the edges of the plant material in as many "repeats" as are necessary. Don't worry if the spray gets on the plant material for after the ink dries it is removed and discarded.

Alternate tricks to use for slightly different effects are to draw the inked brush across a comb or, using the piece of screening, rub your brush back and forth across it holding it about an inch from the paper. As before, a little experimentation will give the desired results.

You may use what colors your artistic sense dictates. Possibly you might want to try mixing colors for special effects or even using two or more colors, with the darker tones being applied first and a drying period allowed between changes.

116

## The Ink Prints

For a different effect, the ink print supplies a variation that is interesting to try. A whole picture of these silhouettes is not difficult to do. Plant material that is quite flat seems to give the best results with this method.

To make these prints, cover the underside of pressed flowers, leaves, ferns, or grasses with printer's ink or India ink. A small brush handles easily or a tamp of cotton on a stick can be improvised. The ink should be distributed as evenly as possible of course. The inked material is then laid, with inked surface uppermost, on a clean working card or paper. Over this place a clean piece of ink paper, being careful not to shift or let it move once it is in contact with the ink. Then, to transfer the ink, rub gently with the finger tips over the material, being careful not to squeeze too much especially at the edges but applying just enough pressure to effect the transfer.

As with the blueprints and spatter prints, faded or less colorful pressings are quite useful and usable for ink prints. There are always Christmas cards to be made, and children can use this method without too much of a mess ensuing.

# DESIGNING THE PICTURES

## The Passe-partout

For picture work, the passe-partout is a method of framing by which glass, picture, and backing are fastened together by means of a tape. The tape is now made with adhesive on its back and it serves as the binding that holds the parts together by being fastened to the top surface, bent over the edge, and pressed on the backing. It is interesting to know that the French term means "that which passes everywhere" and quite specifically a master key. The use of passe-partout for picture work is an old nineteenth-century one, at which time it was very popular. Pictures framed in this way are called passe-partouts.

To frame our pictures by this device, the glass and backing card used are of the same size. On the cardboard, a piece of gold or silver paper of the same size is placed. Because gold and silver backgrounds were once so widely used for this type of framing it is best to follow the tradition and use them where period pieces are desired.

---

### ILLUSTRATION 37

A passe-partout mass arrangement. Pink and blue larkspur, white alyssum, scarlet morning glory, pink azalea, purple pansy, pink columbine, pink polyanthus rose, and white narcissus are combined with foliage of various types. The design is of old French inspiration. Background: gold paper pasted on cardboard; frame: green velvet ribbon glued over the binding tape.

Gold makes an excellent foil for other colors. You will recall that many of the old masters painted on gold backgrounds to set off their foreground colors. During the Italian Renaissance artists used gold lavishly in their ceiling decorations to play up the highly decorated walls and elegant furnishings. Silver has the quality of heightening the color value of neighboring colors. In it there is something of the character of white when used in combination with other colors.

On the chosen background, arrange your dried specimens in whatever design pleases your fancy and lay the glass carefully over it. Inspect for any shifting of material. Fasten on the four sides temporarily with small pieces of masking tape. Then, working carefully, bind the unit with the adhesive-backed tape in whatever color you have selected. Modern tape offers a wide range of colors and sizes to work with. Be sure that the tape is four-square on the glass and is pressed on smoothly all around, front and back, and that the corners are carefully mitered. To make a really handsome period passe-partout use plain tape and cover with velvet ribbon, perhaps with a perky bow at the top.

## The Look-through Picture

For a look-through picture, use glasses for front and back without a background of any kind. The plant materials are affixed to one glass with white of egg (the albumen), very lightly whipped and using just enough to hold in place; glue is applied to the edges all around and the second glass of the same size is then laid over the first. The unit is then bound as a passe-partout. Our picture now can be seen from either side. A massed arrangement, a piece of fern, or just a single spray of flowers looks well when treated in this way. Look-through pictures are very smart in pairs. Need we say watch out for too colorful a wall background?

## Flower Pictures Mounted in Plastic

Paper-thin pressed flowers and foliage can be "framed" between two sheets of clear plastic to make a look-through picture. The Plexiglas and other types of plastic sheets come in several thicknesses and are bonded together for permanence. After mounting the design in the same way as for pictures under glass, you can leave it as is, or it can be finished like the passe-partouts, either plain or fancy as you choose.

The plastic sheets are laminated at the edges with Rex-

N-Glue, a transparent, non-staining cement used for bonding plastic to plastic. This glue, plastic, sheets and Plexiglas may be obtained from Berton Plastics, Inc., 79 Fifth Avenue, New York 3, New York.

# 8. Legends and the Language of Flowers

Because so many pressed-flower pictures have a nostalgic or sentimental association, knowledge of the legends and language of flowers adds to our appreciation of them. Many of these associations are centuries old, and if the recipient of a pressed-flower gift also knows them, or is informed about them by a note, pleasure on both sides is increased.

## Legend of the Chrysanthemum

Kiku-no-hana, whose name means Golden Flower, as the story goes, was a girl-child of wondrous beauty, who lived in the remotest part of China. She spent her days gently wandering among the flowers and musing upon the love she bore for her chosen sweetheart, Kukuri-bana. For he had told her that they must hasten to marry so they might have as many years together as possible. And she wondered how many years this might be, so she asked an elf to tell her truly.

123

Without a moment's thought the elf said, "You will live together as many years as the flower that you shall choose has petals."

But the sad thing was that Kiku-no-hana could find no flowers that had more than five petals, and she became frightened and grieved. Day after day she searched far and wide for a flower that had a multitude of petals. When at last she found one with seventeen, she plucked it quickly. As there was no one to see what she was doing, she took a golden hairpin from her hair and deftly separated each petal into two, then into four—until at last she had a flower with countless petals.

After some months Kiku-no-hana of the many-petaled flower married Kukuri-bana, which means Binding Flower, and from the union of these two came the species of chrysanthemum that has become the ancestors of the many-petalled flowers of our gardens of today.

All through the Far East, the chrysanthemum is the symbol of purity, perfection, and long life.

---

ILLUSTRATION 38

Chrysanthemums in a crescent design made up of small white, pink, and crimson flowers with buds and leaves. The beautiful legend of the chrysanthemum is retold in Chapter 8. Background: pale pink woolen yarn; frame: gold.

124

DESIGNING THE PICTURES

*Legend of the Crocus*

In the land of ancient Greece, this story was told. Crocus was a noble youth who was very much in love with a beautiful shepherdess named Smilax. But the laws of the gods would not permit him to marry her. In bitter disappointment and despair Crocus killed himself. Smilax was heartbroken and wept so piteously that Flora, the goddess of the Flowers and of Spring, took compassion on the sorrowing maiden. Using her powers as a goddess, Flora transformed Crocus into the flower that bears his name and Smilax into a beautiful vine. Thus the marriage that could not take place in life was celebrated in the garlands that were made of the lovely flowers, that spring up each year from the little crocus bulb, and the twining tendrils of the smilax, for these two plants were always used by the ancient Greeks at their marriage festivals. In the language of flowers the crocus means "gladness" and smilax "binding."

---

### ILLUSTRATION 39

A green and yellow mass arrangement in which yellow crocus and celosia are combined with green ferns and grasses on an unusual background. Background: light green woolen yarn with spaced horizontal lines of yarn superimposed; frame: gold.

126

ILLUSTRATION 40

A modern design using narcissus, var. Poetaz. The cluster-type flower of white petals and sepals and shallow yellow cup form part of the decorative pattern. Background: pale green woolen yarn; frame: bamboo. *Courtesy Brooklyn Botanic Garden.*

*Legend of the Dogwood Tree*

This symbolic legend is centuries old. At the time of the crucifixion of Christ, the dogwood tree attained the size of the oak and of the other trees of the forest. So strong and firm was its wood that it was chosen as the timber that made the cross. This was the red dogwood or pricke-timber tree.

To be used thus for such a cruel purpose greatly distressed the tree and Jesus, nailed upon it, sensed this feeling of the tree and in His gentle pity for all sorrow, spoke to it and said: "Because of your regret and pity for my suffering, I make you this promise: Never again shall the dogwood tree grow large enough to be used for a cross. Henceforth it shall be slender and shall be bent and twisted, and its blossoms shall be in the form of a cross with two long and two short petals. And in the center of the outer edge of each petal, there will be nail prints. And in the center of each flower, brown with rust and stained with blood, will be a crown of thorns,—this so that all will remember it was upon a dogwood tree that I was Crucified, and this tree shall not be mutilated nor destroyed but cherished and protected as a reminder of my agony and death upon the Cross."

This was the legend, though in fact there are two dogwood trees, the *Cornus sanguinea* and the *Cornus florida;* the latter is the flowering dogwood we know so well. The name dogwood came from the fact that in ancient times, the berries were used to make a decoction to cure mange on dogs.

By law, in the State of New York, the native dogwood tree may not be uprooted nor the flowers picked for any purpose. Perhaps in your State or locality it is similarly protected, so check before picking the flowers for pressing. Of course if the tree is on your own property you may make use of it for pressed flower pictures.

## Legends of the Narcissus

Ovid, the Latin poet, retells this classic story familiar to almost everyone. The story-myth comes from ancient Greece and tells of the son of Cephissus and Leirope who was named Narcissus and for whom it was predicted that he would have a long and happy life as his lot was decreed by the Fates, provided that he never gazed upon his own features. It happened one day that in his wanderings he chanced to see his reflection in a quiet water pool, and in a moment of human vanity, he fell in love with his own image. The Fates saw to it that his punishment was meted out and he soon pined away and died. On the very spot where he died, there soon sprang from the earth the beau-

130

tiful nodding flower which thereafter was called after him, narcissus.

Another legend tells how the beautiful but vain youth Narcissus spurned the love of the nymph Echo, who pined away until nothing was left but her voice. And Nemesis in revenge for Echo's plight caused the vain youth to fall in love with his own reflection and so to die.

But the Roman historian Pliny holds to another story. He said that the name came from the Greek word *narke* and referred to the narcotic or hypnotic perfume of the flower. The narcissus was the flower consecrated to the Furies, the three goddesses of vengeance, who used the flowers to stupify those whom they wished to punish. The odor of the flower has been said to cause hallucinations according to other ancient writers.

Many names have been used for this lovely flower. An old English name is Lent lily, for there it blooms in the Lenten season. It has also been called the chalice flower, from the resemblance of its corona to the chalice used for the sacramental wine.

Have you thought of a spring picture in a slim line arrangement made of Scotch broom, a few grape hyacinths, a narcissus bud, a half-opened flower and a fully opened one? Try one, for it will make a charming gift for the one-who-has-everything.

DESIGNING THE PICTURES

## *The Language of Flowers*

I have seen in a modern book a list of flowers—almost five hundred are given—which have associated with them what is called their sentimental philology; it is amusing if not instructive. But it is difficult to understand some of the associations for they seem incompatible with the flower if not grossly misrepresentative of it. I prefer the list given below, which is taken from a quaint old book called *The Flower Vase*. It was first issued in 1844, and belonged to my grandmother. Search your own memory and you may well recall that you did find a special meaning in that first red rose from your swain. Sentiment, yes, but sentimentality, never!

The flowers, shrubs, and trees and their sentiments are given, together with the sentimental philology from the longer list (in parenthesis) where it differs from or adds to the older association.

| | |
|---|---|
| Acacia | Platonic love (friendship) |
| Alyssum | Worth beyond beauty (exemplary modesty) |

ILLUSTRATION 41

"The Language of Flowers." An engraving expressively made for *Godey's Lady's Book* (1840-1870) by W. E. Tucker. Exact date unknown, but probably in the late 1840's as this was a period of great interest in the subject.

THE LANGUAGE OF FLOWERS

## DESIGNING THE PICTURES

| | |
|---|---|
| Amaranth | Immortality |
| Anemone | Frailty (fading hope) |
| Apple blossom | Fame speaks you great and good (immortality) |
| Ash | Grandeur (prudence, with me you are safe) |
| Aster | Beauty in retirement |
| Bachelor's button | Hope in love (celibacy, hope is lost) |
| Balm | Sweets of social intercourse (sympathy) |
| Balm of Gilead | I am cured |
| Balsam | Impatience |
| Barberry | Petulence (sharpness of temper) |
| Bay leaf | I change but in dying (in death) |
| Birch | Gracefulness |
| Bindweed | Humility |
| Blue bell | Constancy (sorrowful regret) |
| Box | Stoicism |
| Broome | Neatness (humility) |
| Burdock | Importunity |
| Calla | Feminine modesty (beauty, maiden modesty) |
| Chamomile | Energy in adversity |
| Candytuft | Indifference |
| Cardinal flower | Distinction |
| Carnation | Pride |
| Catchfly | Snare (pretended love) |
| Cedar tree | Spiritual strength (think of me; I live but for thee) |
| Cherry blossom | Spiritual beauty |
| China aster | Your sentiments meet with a return (afterthoughts) |

134

# LEGENDS AND THE LANGUAGE OF FLOWERS

| | |
|---|---|
| Chrysanthemum | A heart left to desolation (dejection) |
| Cinquefoil | Love constant but hopeless (maternal affection) |
| Clematis | Mental excellence (mental beauty) |
| Columbine | I cannot give thee up (desertion, folly, inconstancy) |
| Cowslip | Native grace (winning grace, comliness) |
| Coreopsis | Always cheerful |
| Coriander | Concealed merit (hidden worth) |
| Cypress | Disappointed hopes (despair, mourning) |
| Dahlia | Elegance and dignity (forever thine) |
| Daisy | Beauty and innocence |
| Dandelion | Coquetry (love's oracle) |
| Dew-plant | A serenade |
| Elder | Compassion (zealousness) |
| Eglantine | Poetry (intent, I wound to heal) |
| Everlasting | Always remembering |
| Evergreen | Poverty and worth |
| Fir | Time |
| Flowering reed | Confidence in Heaven |
| Forget-me-not | True love (constancy) |
| Foxglove | I am not ambitious for myself, but for you (youth, insincerity) |
| Fuchsia | Humble love (confiding love, taste) |
| Gentian | Virgin pride (sweet be thy love) |
| Geranium, Rose | Preference |
| Scarlet | Thou art changed (comforting) |
| Oak | True friendship |
| Lemon | Tranquillity of mind (unexpected meeting) |

135

DESIGNING THE PICTURES

| | |
|---|---|
| Silvered-leaved | Recall |
| Gilly flower | Lasting beauty (bonds of affection, she is fair) |
| Goldenrod | Encouragement (precaution) |
| Hawthorn | Hope |
| Heliotrope | Devotion (eagerness) |
| Hibiscus | Beauty in vain (delicious beauty) |
| Hollyhock | Ambition (fruitfulness) |
| Honeysuckle | Fidelity (hands of love) |
| Hydrangea | Heartfulness (a boaster) |
| Ice-plant | Your looks freeze me (an old beau, rejected) |
| Iris | A message (my compliments) |
| Ivy | I have found one true heart (fidelity, friendship, wedded love) |
| Jasmine | Amiability |
| Jonquil | Affection returned (can you return my love? I desire a return of affection) |
| King-cup | I wish I was rich |
| Lady's slipper | Capricious beauty (win and wear me) |
| Larkspur | Inconstancy (fickleness, haughtiness) |
| Laurel | Virtue is true beauty (treachery) |
| Lavender | Acknowledgment (distrust) |
| Lilac | First emotion of love (fastidiousness) |
| Lily | Purity (sweetness) |
| Lily-of-the-valley | Heart withering in secret (perfect purity) |
| Locust | Affection beyond the grave |
| Lupine | Dejection (fanciful, always happy) |
| London pride | Frivolity |
| Mallow | Sweet disposition (mildness) |

136

| | |
|---|---|
| Maple | Reserve (retirement) |
| Marigold | Contempt (cruelty in love, inquietude) |
| Mignonette | Moral beauty (your qualities surpass your charm) |
| Mimosa | Sensitiveness (exquisite, fastidious) |
| Nasturtium | Patriotism |
| Nightshade | Dark thoughts (your thoughts are dark) |
| Oak | Hospitality |
| Oleander | Beware |
| Pansy | Tender and pleasant thoughts (think of me) |
| Passion flower | Religious fervor (holy love) |
| Pea, Everlasting | Wilt thou go? (appoint a meeting) |
| Sweet | Departure (remember) |
| Peach blossom | I am your captive |
| Petunia | Thou art less proud than they deem thee (you soothe me) |
| Peony | Ostentation (anger, indignation) |
| Phlox | Our souls are united (unanimity) |
| Pine | Time and faith (pity) |
| Pink, White | Lovely and pure affection (fascination, talent) |
| Red | Women's love (ardent love) |
| Polyanthus | Confidence (purse proud) |
| Poppy (white) | Forgetfulness |
| Primrose | Modest worth (believe me, youth and sadness) |
| Primrose, Evening | I am more faithful than thou (inconstancy) |
| Rose-bud | Confession of love |

## DESIGNING THE PICTURES

| | |
|---|---|
| Rose, Bridal | Happy love |
| Burgundy | Simplicity beauty (unconscious beauty) |
| Damask | Bashful love (young and brilliant) |
| Moss | Superior merit |
| Multiflora | Grace |
| White | Too young to love (I am worthy of you, silence) |
| Red-leaved | Diffidence |
| Sage | Domestic virtues |
| Snapdragon | Dazzling but dangerous (presumption, no) |
| Snowball | Thoughts of Heaven (bound) |
| Snowdrop | I am not a summer friend (friendship in trouble, hope) |
| Star of Bethlehem | Let us follow Jesus (atonement) |
| Sumack | Splendid misery (I shall survive the change) |
| Sunflower | Smile on me still (you are splendid) |
| Sweet William | Gallantry (grant me one smile) |
| Syringa | Memory (you shall be happy yet) |
| Thistle | Never forget (austerity) |
| Tulip | Beautiful eyes (your eyes are beautiful) |
| Verbena | Sensibility (tender and quick emotion) |
| Violet | Faithfulness (love) |
| Water lily | Eloquence (purity of heart) |
| Willow | Forsaken |
| Witch hazel | A spell (mysticism, inspiration) |
| Woodbine | Fraternal love |
| Yarrow | A cure for the heartache |
| Zinnia | I mourn your absence (thoughts of absent friends) |

138

...lorful if a bit unusual; if you like water cress, you mig...
...y this too.

THE GERANIUM. The geranium is widely distribute... ...roughout the temperate and subtropical zones. Its origi... ...al habitat was South Africa and there are more than ...hree hundred and fifty species in the family, which is of ...he genus *Pelargonium*. In some areas this name is used ...for the geranium. The many bright colors usually dry ...true to color. Cranesbill is the quaint name for a wild- ...flower in this family.

THE ZINNIA. *Zinnia elegans,* the common garden flower, ...comes to use from tropical America and is named after ...one Johann Gottfried Zinn, a noted German botanist. ...There are a number of varieties and many hybrids. Its ...soubriquets of youth-and-old-age and cut-and-come-again ...are not too often heard these days. Gay and colorful, ...though scentless, it provides plenty of color for dried ...specimens.

THE MARIGOLD. The marigold supposedly derives its ...name from the Virgin Mary, but as there are a number of ...plants called marigold—the pot-marigold, the bur-mari- ...gold, marsh-marigold, fetid marigold, water marigold ...among them—we must rely on legend that it was the pot- ...marigold or calendula that the Virgin wore on her bosom. ...The familiar garden marigold in all its varieties bears the

## Oddments on Sundry Matters

Popular lore about plants and flowers is often reflected in ancient customs, and searching for such material is truly a hobby in its own right. To me, knowing the background of my picture and its material has always had a certain fascination and has added to the pleasure of making the picture. A few interesting things I have come upon in making and using pressed flowers may suggest possibilities to those who wish to make a hobby of such research. To begin with there is the crocus.

THE CROCUS. The crocus was alleged in olden times to have many fine properties. For example, used in the prep- aration of drinks, doubtless an infusion in wine, it gave a perpetual protection from headache and indigestion. Fine too was it for the heart and lungs when properly prepared and administered. Ancient physicians thought it useful in time of pestilence and plague as a medicinal preventative. One variety, the autumn crocus, is the source of a widely used flavoring, the saffron of the Medi- terrean world. It was also used as a deodorant in Grecian theaters and public places. And it was noted as one of the two things that "corrupt" women, the other being gold. The dried yellow stamens provide this rare item of com- merce!

## DESIGNING THE PICTURES

THE VIOLET. In ancient Athens, the violet was combined with the carnation in garlands for weddings and high ceremonial occasions, a combination as socially necessary as that of crocus and smilax. It too had a place among the medicinal herbs, for it was said that a compress of violets, strawberries and poppy seeds would assuredly cure sick headaches and sleeplessness. Old herbals attest to the modest violet's curative powers. Violets are still today candied and eaten, but as a delicacy rather than for any curative powers they might have.

THE NASTURTIUM. Since 1684, the nasturtium from Mexico and South America has been cultivated in England, and by a mix-up in names has been given the same name as one of the local members of the cress family, and so it is called there Indian Cress. Its true family name is *Tropaeolum,* but only the botanist knows it as such. Its lovely colorful flowers, tender leaves, and sharp-flavored green seedpods are quite edible but of rather doubtful use at the meeting of the garden club. The seeds are also pickled and used as capers are used. A nasturtium salad is

ILLUSTRATION 42

Nasturtium buds and flowers in shades and tints of yellow, orange, and red against the shield-like leaves give unusual texture and color to this design. Background: light gray construction paper; frame: maple.

family name of *Tagetes* and if you ask for this plant from your seedman you are likely to get a tiny-flowered lemon-scented fine-leaved variety, *T. minuta*. It is a very good garden plant indeed. These flowers originally came from Mexico, although they are best known as French marigolds where they have long been hybridized as small-flowered plants, or as African or Aztec marigolds, if they are the tall large-flowered plants (known respectively as *T. patula* and *T. erecta*). The color range is from palest lemon to deep mahogany and also occurs in various mixtures. A good picture-making plant.

THE HONEYSUCKLE. In medieval gardens, the honeysuckle was ever present, for no lady of the time would be without the distilled Flower Water for which the blossoms of this plant were considered so essential. The water, pleasantly perfumed, was used also as a vehicle for the more distasteful medicinal herbs used in those times. The sweet blossoms themselves were considered to have a wholesome, therapeutic value. Long ago country people in many lands thought that the crushed leaves of this plant when applied to bee stings would draw off much of the soreness.

THE ROSE. Throughout the course of time the rose has been a universal favorite among the flowers and seems to have won fairly its attribute of "the queen of all flowers."

143

DESIGNING THE PICTURES

From the rose comes attar of rose which is the essential oil base for the manufacture of perfumes of all kinds. It is the petals of certain varieties of the rose that supply this essential oil, the damask rose being one important type. Whole areas in the Balkans are devoted to the growing of the rose for this commercially valuable product for export to perfume makers everywhere. There is an ancient tax record, dated A.D. 210, which shows that the province of Bagdad in Mesopotamia was required to supply thirty thousand jars of rose water annually. The rose hip has been used for centuries for a conserve, and during World War II there was revival of this delicacy in England, owing to a shortage of other fruits. Candied rose petals are elegant edible decorations for cakes and such. As you know, the rose petal is the principal ingredient of the potpourri.

THE ANEMONE. The lovely anemone, crimson-flowered because it sprang from the blood of Adonis whose Semitic name of Na'man it bears, was grown as a plant novelty in

ILLUSTRATION 43

A panel of garden flowers using purple loosestrife, pink coxcomb, blue, purple and yellow pansy, mimosa, pink rose, pink geranium, purple larkspur, purple salvia, rose heather, yellow celosia, blue hydrangea, and lavender hosta, combined with various leaves and ferns. Background: cream-colored flannel; frame: white and gold.

the garden of an early Egyptian pharaoh, thousands of years ago. Pharaoh's ancient gardener must have secured the plant from its habitat in the Orient. The Romans were well aware that it was the favorite flower of the goddess Venus and so they too appreciated it. From the Netherlands came the anemone to be grown in the first Dutch gardens of New Amsterdam in the New World, for it is mentioned in the records of those earliest of American gardens.

THE HOLLYHOCK. The hollyhock from China was an early arrival too in American gardens. In 1672, one John Josselyn published a list of flowers, herbs, and vegetables growing in the gardens of his time and reported the hollyhock as thriving well.

THE ACACIA. The acacia, a native of Asia and Africa, and the mimosa, native to Asia and Africa but also to Mexico and Australia, are close kin. Acacia was the Greek name for the Egyptian species, and albizzia is the name by which many of the mimosa are now known. You may know it by its popular name of silk-tree. Cultivated varieties have an exceptionally wide variety of uses in commerce. One species is grown in the perfume centers of France at Cannes and Grasse; there the flowers are used in the making of violet perfume, as that is the odor of the flower. The leaves of some species are used in the culinary

146

arts for flavoring. Other products are dyes, medicines, gum arabic, soap- and hair-wash ingredients, and bark for the tanning of leathers. The wood is used for fuel and fence posts, known as wattle, and that of several species is used for fine cabinet work and furniture.

# *Part* III
## SEED AND CITRUS-SKIN DECORATION

# 9. Decorating with Seeds and Fruit Forms

Mary, Mary, quite contrary, planted her seeds all in a row. The flowers that were to grow from these seeds would delight her eye and ours by their beautiful colors and shapes and textures. But all too often we forget that the very seeds which are behind the flowering plant, so to speak, have a remarkable character of their own. They are as varied in form and shape and color and texture as are the flowers. While seeds of assorted kinds have for centuries been strung as necklaces, amulets, ear dangles and used for adornment of the human body, however very limited use has been made of seeds for purely decorative art purposes. Only in recent years has the infinite variety of the seed-world become recognized as a source of natural materials for creating beautiful pictures.

Seed is a generic word. It includes the dustlike seed of the begonia and petunia—two million of the latter to an ounce, we are told—as well as the giant forty-pound coconut. Nature has been uncanny in choosing ways to make

151

it possible for seeds to survive and begin a new life in the world of flora and fauna.

*Seeds in Variety*

As the form of seed is often a matter of adaptation to a viable means of distribution, some of the more unusual forms are worth noting. Every flower grower recognizes those of the garden plants, such as the violet and balsam whose seed head pops open and scatters the matured seed broadcast, the poppy capsule that holds its seed burden until some strong wind bends the dried head and deposits its contents nearby, and the many plants that let their seed fall as it may. There are those seeds that are wind-borne, as the dandelion and milkweed and lace vine, with their little parachutes that carry them afar. The winged form of the maple and tuliptree seeds is another way in which seed is carried by the wind away from the parent to some open spot. Animals distribute many seeds that are equipped with burrs, like the chestnut and dock, or hooks, like the unicorn, that catch in the animal's coat and travel afar before falling to the ground. Hard-coated seed and grains are adapted by nature to survive the digestive processes of many animals and birds and so their transport is accomplished. The coconut is often water-borne and travels thousands of miles in ocean currents to be washed upon some distant shore. The ubiquitous squirrel and other rodents do their share by burying nuts they cannot store and then forgetting them.

Then there are seeds that lie dormant for hundreds of years, buried deep in the earth like sleeping princesses until the moment comes when they are exposed to some form of the oxygen that is necessary for their sprouting. The lotus seed has this extraordinary characteristic and archeologists are constantly finding others that have persisted with germinal life through milleniums.

Most seeds have a kind of rest period after maturing on the plant before germination takes place and that is when we catch them unawares for our purposes, so different from Nature's. Here is a list of seed material that can be used in making seed pictures, mosaics, plaques, and other decorative articles:

THE CONES. Alder, cedrus Atlantica, cypress, Douglas fir, hemlock, pinyon pine, white pine, redwood, sequoia, spruce, tamarack.

THE NUTS. Acorn, almond, brazilnut, cashew, chestnut, hazelnut, peanut, pecan, walnut.

THE FRUIT PITS. Apricot, avocado, cherry, date, nectarine, peach, plum.

THE BEANS. Coffee, hyacinth, scarlet runner, those from the grocery store (see below).

## SEED AND CITRUS-SKIN DECORATION

THE FRUIT AND VEGETABLE SEED. Acorn squash, artichoke, butternut squash, grapefruit, honeydew melon, hubbard squash, lemon, lime, muskmelon, orange, pumpkin, watermelon, zucchini.

THE SEEDS OF FLOWERING PLANTS, TREES, AND SHRUBS. Albizzia, althea, apple, azalea, bittersweet, bottlebush, date palm, euonymous, gingko, gourd, gum ball, hemerocallis, hibiscus, hollyhock, honesty, iris, Job's tear, lathyrus, lilac, lupin, milkweed, mountain ash, mullein, osage orange, pear, pokeberry, pomegranate, poppy, prayer bead, rose hip, sunflower, sorghum, tulip, witch hazel.

THE PODS. Ailanthus, black and honey locust, castor bean, catalpa, cotton, eucalyptus, Hawaiian lip stick, jacaranda, lotus, magnolia, okra, pagoda, stericula, trumpet vine, unicorn, wild iris, wisteria, yucca.

COMMERCIALLY DRIED FOODS. Allspice, barley, beans (black-eyed, fava, kidney, lima, marrow, navy, pink,

---

### ILLUSTRATION 44

A seed plaque whose inspiration was an ornamental design by Pillemont (1728-1808) in the Metropolitan Museum of Art, New York. The seeds used: fava, kidney, and pinto beans, hubbard and butternut squash, pumpkin, muskmelon, honeydew melon, green pea, chickpea, lentil, sorghum, mustard, peppercorn, gourd, apple, althea, honesty, locust, and barley; the stems: small twigs. The colors: tan, brown, black, gray, white, cream, and green. Background: maple-stained plywood, plastic-sprayed. Everything is glued on.

pinto), cassia, clove, mustard seed, peas (split green and yellow, crushed, chick), peppercorn, popcorn, rice, strawberry and Indian corn.

These lists contain some—by no means all—of the seeds that you can use in dried form. Your own garden will undoubtedly supply you with a number more that have definite possibilities. There are many wild plants with unusual seed heads that can be collected and dried, such things as pencil-sized cattails and fern fronds. Sea oats, agave clusters, and the Hawaiian wood rose are perhaps not as easily obtainable as are some of the pods listed above, but you will have many seeds about you at one time or other during the year, so save them for later use. Yes, even those that turn up in your kitchen.

For the more exotic seeds, pods, and cones, a local florist often has them for sale, for he too recognizes their decorative values in flower arrangements. A very large selection of such material can be obtained from "Treasures of the Sea and Land" at 1458 State Street, Schenectady, New York. This house specializes in unusual items from the desert, mountain, prairie, and seashore areas.

*What To Decorate with Seed*

There is actually a limitless number of things that can be decorated with seed forms. Elaborate or simple as you choose, your decorated pieces should be conceived in terms of design and muted colors, with seed form as the basic element. Don't hesitate to try and copy from another art form that pleases you, whether it is an interesting drawn work pattern from an heirloom towel, a design in gesso on a box or picture frame, or just something you saw in a magazine advertisement. You can decorate wood panels and plaques, Lazy Susans, boxes, bookends, scrapbook covers, small albums, pins and buttons on a wooden base, matchbox covers and countless other items. Wood bases can be homemade or purchased.

In making panels and plaques, all kinds of wood are suitable, for example, mahogany, maple, birch, pine, walnut, cedar and cypress shakes, and teak.

*The Basic Method of Using Seed for Decoration*

The first step concerns the wooden base. The wood must be sand-papered until it is perfectly smooth on the surfaces to be decorated (except the shakes). (If desired, stain can be applied before shellacking.) To seal the pores of the wood brush on a coating of white shellac, white shellac remember, for this will give a proper surface for the glue to adhere to. Dry overnight and as much longer as is needed for the surface to become thoroughly dry and smooth. A sticky coating will ruin all your good work.

157

SEED AND CITRUS-SKIN DECORATION

Next, assemble all the material you are going to use (see the list at the end of the chapter): seed collection, bits of dried twigs for stems, tweezers for tiny pieces, a small brush, glue pot, a sketch of your design if you are not working freehand, a tiny spatula for removing unwanted or misplaced glue. The very small seed can be kept in small boxes or in a glass painter's mixing-dish or in water-color pans.

While assembling your materials you have doubtless been thinking of your design and have chosen one, as discussed in Chapter 3. Using your cones, nuts, pits, seeds, and whatever, lay out your pattern piece by piece on the background board just as you wish it to appear. If, for example, you are making a diamond design, all the seeds will be in place in this layout arranged for contrast in shape, size, color and texture.

Then lift each piece by hand or tweezer and drop a tiny spot of glue in its place on the board and replace the

ILLUSTRATION 45

A seed arrangement in the Japanese manner. The base is of crushed dried green peas; the container of long-grained rice; the flowers of honeydew melon seed with mustard seed center; lower leaves of seed pods of wild primrose; the branches are from the pagoda tree. Background: light-colored wood panel, laced with plastic, all plastic-sprayed. Everything is glued on.

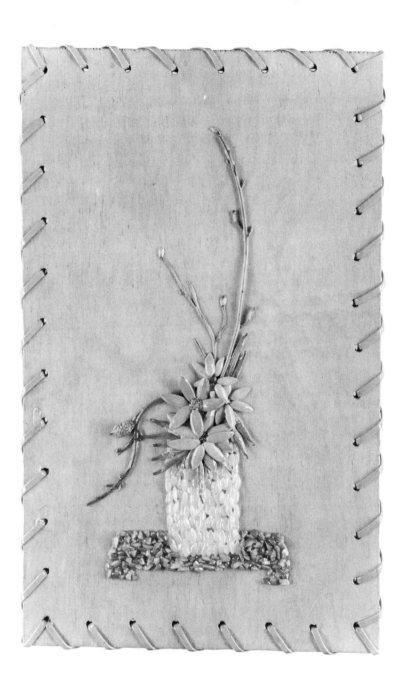

seed on the glue, pressing it firmly down. Remove at once any glue that has exuded, before it has a chance to harden. These small spots of glue usually harden quickly, so always keep your board clean. Continue piece by piece until the design is completely glued in place. Let dry thoroughly, at least twenty-four hours, before handling.

The last step is to coat the entire design with shellac or varnish; again use the white, colorless kinds, or you can use clear plastic spray. You may use a brush for this job or spray it on. The handy aerosol spray cans that are available are useful here. Be sure that every nook and cranny is coated but very, very lightly and evenly. A second coat is necessary and a third coat desirable to give the work a finished appearance.

No doubt a time will come when it will be necessary to dust your plaque. For this use a fine soft brush to flick away the dust. All seed-work should be treated this way.

*A Seed Mosaic*

Many of you have seen the glorious Byzantine mosaic work pictured in art books and occasionally on Christmas cards. A handicraft using similar materials is now quite popular for table tops, bowls, ashtrays, and the like. But have you considered seed mosaics? As decorative pictures for a mantlepiece or as wall pieces, seed mosaics and murals are unusual, with unique charm. Because a mosaic has a rather flat surface, the seed material should be relatively of similar size but with considerable variation in color tone; the rather pebbly surface provides the shadows.

After selecting the material you are going to use in sufficient quantity for the size you are making, prepare the background. This may be a piece of heavy posterboard, which is less expensive than plywood. Any thin, flat board may be used of course. In either case the surface must be sanded smooth so that the whole design may be penciled on it. Work on the design a small portion at a time, spreading glue and placing seeds of various colors and shapes so that there are only minor variations in size. The background, using only one kind of seed, is filled in after the design has set. Modern designs are attractive presented in this way; even realistic scenes are possible after some experimental trial-and-error work.

## The Seed Mural

Using the same techniques as for seed mosaics, you can create murals that are very beautiful and that will fit into any scheme of decoration. The difference between the mural and the mosaic is that in making a mural you have a greater freedom in surface texture. The penciled sketch is made on the background as before, and the processing is the same. But instead of rather shallow, flat pieces, all kinds of seeds, pods, nuts, cones, and twigs can be used, whatever best fulfills the requirements of the design and its size. In the making of a mural, let your imagination go to work. Murals are fascinating and the results rewarding, so just be your own artist, using rather unconventional materials.

*Framing*

Panels and plaques are most often left unframed. With their interesting texture and depth they really look their best without the distraction that a frame often provides. Other seed pieces can be framed or not, as you choose. If no frame is used, then be sure that the edges of the piece are neatly regular.

If you decide to frame, here is one way of doing it. Select a frame you think is suitable—the natural wood, rather broad-shouldered frames used for modern oil paintings are a good choice—and cut your background wood to exact size to fit the bevel at the back; then secure it firmly with nails until it is rigid. Now, working on the front side build your picture as before. Glass is not used in framing this type of picture as a rule.

There is an exception and that is the shadow box. Glass-enclosed shadow boxes (that once contained nine-

162

teenth-century hair and floral wreaths, dried bouquets, compositions of nuts, seed, shells and even of feathers, as well as large gilt-framed photographs) are attractive period pieces. They make stunning decorations when they are used to hold modern seed mosaics and murals. Just be sure that you have given plenty of thought to how one is going to look in its new surroundings before going ahead. Shadow boxes are not inexpensive nor are they always easy to come by.

*What You Need To Make Seed Pictures*

Before you begin making a seed picture you want to have on hand the following equipment:

Backgrounds—wood panels, card, or posterboard.

Seeds—a large collection and wide selection of many kinds.

Adhesive—any good glue with body.

Scissors and shears—for cutting and trimming.

Tweezers—for handling small pieces.

Spatula—for removing excess glue.

Sandpaper—fine gauge, for sanding background woods.

Stains—for coloring natural woods if desired.

Fixative—white shellac or varnish, in plain or aerosol can. Clear plastic spray is also good. Yellow shellac

163

or varnish darkens with age; white in old, opened cans does also.

Brushes—for applying stain or shellac, and for dusting
Weights—sometimes needed to hold down stems or twigs, small flat stones are useful.

*Note:* If you stain the background, apply one coat with a coat of shellac to seal. If it is already the desired color, you will need only to sand and shellac as described.

# 10. Decorations with Citrus Skins

Sometimes we amaze ourselves by discovering what can be done with material that is normally disposed of as waste. So I conclude that there is beauty and some usefulness in almost everything if we will only look for it.

For me there is great charm in citrus fruit skins, the peel of the grapefruit, the orange, lemon and the lime. I have found other ways to use them besides for candied peel or grating on foods for flavoring.

Eye-catching wall panels and plaques can be made from the trimmed and dried peel of these citrus fruits. They can be made in any size and with any kind of wood background. Dried peels make attractive decorations for the straw, plastic, and burlap bags that are so popular today. Christmas tree ornaments are another possibility. Dried peels that have been shaped and painted brilliantly in gold or silver or other bright colors become intriguing decorative pieces for your tree or for a table arrangement.

## SEED AND CITRUS-SKIN DECORATION

So far, I know of no one else who has used citrus peels for decorative purposes.

Here is my method.

### The Preparation of the Skins

As might be expected, the fruit is halved and the juice extracted or the pulp segments removed. Then all membranous matter is removed carefully. When you have done this you will find a network of fine lines that seem to make a pattern. I often wonder how many have ever seen this internal structural design; like the steel skeleton behind the masonry walls of a building, it exists unseen and unknown except to very few of us.

The skins are then rinsed well in cold water; holding them under running water is better than dunking them in a basin. In this state they are ready to be cut into shapes to be used in a design. Using a pair of sharp scissors or shears, cut out shapes that resemble whole flowers, petals or leaves, and stems. The pattern to follow may be marked on the skin with a soft pencil, or you may simply use a practiced eye in a freehand approach. Think of the flowers as having five, seven, or nine petals and make the leaves of assorted shapes. Enough skins should be available at each processing to give an adequate number of pieces to be used for your designs. The dried forms will

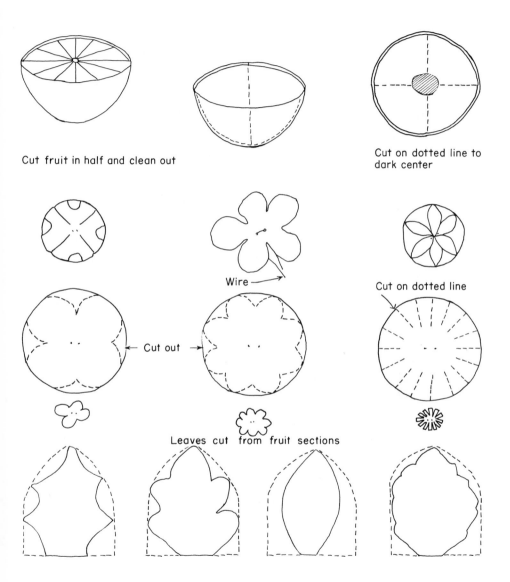

Cut fruit in half and clean out

Cut on dotted line to dark center

Wire

Cut on dotted line

← Cut out →

Leaves cut from fruit sections

Fig. 10   Cutting citrus fruit skins

keep, so make more rather than less than you think you will need. Not only flowers but all sorts of designs can be made, such as stars, tiny angels, Santa Clauses, circles, squares, crescents, fans, rings—any solid shape will do.

Whenever you plan to use the dried pieces in such a way that they will require sewing, as for bags, or wiring, as for tree decorations, make two small holes in the center portion. For hanging shapes the hole is placed near the top of the form.

Drying comes next. A gas oven with a pilot light is ideal, but if you lack a pilot control, you will have to adjust as closely as possible to this heat level. Too warm an oven causes the pieces to brown and become too brittle. Trial and error will eventually give you the right answer.

With pilot-light control, twenty-four hours of drying time will work out about right. Without this control and the oven at its lowest possible heat without danger of going out, four or five hours may be sufficient, but the skins must be inspected frequently because of the faster drying. The oven door is kept closed in either method.

Don't be surprised, when the pieces are removed from the baking, to find that the heat has done some shaping for you and has produced lovely artistic twists and curves.

*Preserving the Skins*

Those pieces that you want to use for wall panels in the natural colors should be coated all over with a clear plastic or varnish spray. Or they may be hand-brushed with clear white shellac. For spraying, a number of pieces can be put in a box and done at one time; for hand brushing, piece by piece is the rule. Never use shellac that has been previously opened or exposed to air frequently; such shellac will stay sticky for a long time or may never even dry at all. So buy in as small a can or jar as possible. For the sprays, read the directions carefully and only use them in well-ventilated rooms and away from pilot lights of any kind. These materials are highly volatile, as you know.

A face mask is helpful for those who are allergic to paint fumes, but there are some people who simply cannot use the spray method at all. Hand-brushing is their lot, and they should use the shellac. Above I have stressed white shellac, because it will not darken the fruit skin and, indeed, it often emphasizes the patterns of the skins somewhat. Orange shellac will darken the skins and will get deeper as it gets older, so only use it if you really want very dark color.

When clear natural color is not wanted, then spray enamels can be used, if you find suitable colors. The range

169

of colors available in spray enamel is not large. Otherwise, paint with can enamel somewhat thinned out. The processing is the same.

*Various Coloring Ideas*

For tree and wreath ornaments, apply spray varnish before you create your ornament. Then, before the varnish is wholly dry sprinkle the pieces of skin with a metallic powder, in any color you desire, or with metallic glitters of gold, silver, copper, and other colors. Both of these are available before the Christmas season in stores of many kinds, and in some all year round. They come in small bottles with shaker tops and so are quite easy to apply. If you prefer not to use solid colors, then designs can be painted on the peels. Imitate conventional patterns or be as original as you want to. The results are striking and different in either case, since your material is so unusual. Even the children can help with the decoration, as they used to do and I hope still do with the coloring and decorating of traditional Easter eggs.

For gift-box tops, bag decorations and other package designs, definite color schemes of complementary colors that match or contrast with background colors can be worked out. Monochromatic schemes are truly effective. Handpainting gives the best results and is easy to do even

170

though you pretend you are not an artist. Be original with a non-seasonal gift package. You'll want less of the holiday tinsel and more subtlety and humor in your design. Abstract, realistic, modern, and traditional designs are all possible with this material.

*Decorating Panels, Plaques, and Woodenware*

All kinds of woods can be used for panels and plaques, but plywood is useful because it is light in weight, it cuts easily into various sizes and shapes, it takes various finishes well, and it is relatively inexpensive compared to fine pieces of cabinet wood. Wooden bowls, shaped canape trays, and pressed wood plates are among the woodenware items that can be effectively decorated.

The same general treatment of the wood is required for citrus fruit decorations as it is for the seed work described in the preceding chapter. Sanding and sealing is necessary, if the natural color is to be used. If other background finishes are desired then staining is done after sanding and before sealing with a varnish, shellac, or plastic spray. A porous surface absorbs too much of the adhesive and, as a slightly different method is used in gluing the citrus fruit pieces in place, proper sealing of the surface obviates the difficulty nicely.

After the wood is properly prepared, plan your design.

## SEED AND CITRUS-SKIN DECORATION

Make a sketch of the pattern to be followed in placing the pieces or, if you prefer, lay out the pieces in such a manner that you have the skins completely worked in their final position. Flower designs in the natural colors are the best for this type of work; although colored work is also possible, it seems less rich and interesting and more artificial than the natural tints and shades.

With design completed, each piece is spotted with the glue or adhesive on the portion that will be in contact with the background; a similar spot of glue is daubed on the wood surface in the place where the skin is to go in the design. Allow to become slightly tacky if that is the glue-maker's direction. (Some glues work best this way.) Then place the skin in position and press firmly. Continue piece by piece until the design is completed.

For the flower centers an accent of some kind is needed. Small seeds or dried material such as barley, corn, peppercorns, cloves, or split peas are ideal. Choose from the lists

---

### ILLUSTRATION 46

A plaque of dried citrus fruits in which orange, grapefruit, lemon, and lime processed peels are cut into petal and leaf shapes and are arranged as flower forms, with seed from mountain ash, barley, dried green peas, and pokeberry seed as the centers. Rose hips are used along the edges. Background: walnut-stained plywood. Everything is glued in place.

172

of seed material in the previous chapter or use any other small and interesting bits you may have collected.

The drying period for the glue is about twenty-four hours. A coating of shellac, varnish, or plastic, brushed on or sprayed, is the next step for the entire piece. Another drying period, another coating, again the drying, and a third coat is applied. You may have noticed that the skins seem to have absorbed a great deal of the first coatings, hence the three coats are necessary to give a fine smooth surface finish, both for appearance and for later ease of cleaning by dusting gently with a soft brush. Now stand aside and admire your handiwork!

An interesting variation in finish is worth trying, for I am sure you will want to make something special for that anniversary or birthday, or just for the fun of it. By coating your designs with brilliant gold or silver or copper spray, you can create smart and handsome decorations with a look. The preparation of the design is the same, but instead of the three coats of varnish or shellac two coats of these metallic sprays are all that is necessary, as the sprays are somewhat heavier. The same periods of drying time are needed for these sprays.

## Banana Skins and Red Pepper

Certainly the skins of bananas and peppers cannot be classed as citrus fruit, but they too can be dried for decorative purposes. Their final shapes and texture after drying make them very worthwhile to try. The pilot-light heat method above described is used for these skins. About twelve to fifteen hours are needed for the banana, while the Italian red peppers, used whole, require about thirty-six hours of drying time. If you do not have the pilot-light control, don't forget to check frequently during the drying process as a much shorter time will be needed. The heat will do the shaping for you. The red peppers develop a lovely texture with a smooth, glossy appearance and unusual twists and curves that make them especially interesting. The red bell peppers will require from ten to fourteen days depending on size, thickness, etc. All are treated in the same way as the citrus skins.

## The Problems of Storage

As with the pressed flowers, small insects will often put in an appearance and work their way into any dried citrus material that has been placed in storage boxes. Here again, moth balls or crystals usually forestall their depredations, so do not neglect this protection.

## SEED AND CITRUS-SKIN DECORATION

Properly protected, your dried citrus fruit pieces and the finished panels and plaques and other decorations will last and continue to give pleasure for a number of years.

### On the Subject of Varnishes and Sprays

While I have used certain brands in my work, there are many on the market that are equally useful. As the varnishes, shellacs, and sprays are manufactured by many makers for local distribution under different brand names, you will undoubtedly find that these work quite as well as those I have tried. Consult your paint supplier, if you have any doubt.

Among those that I have used are the Damar varnishes and lacquers, Bromo Spray-it-yourself Plastic Preservative (a high-luster spray) and Red Devil quick-drying enamels. It may also be, that atmospheric conditions may make a given brand better for use in one locality than another and manufacturers may have taken it into consideration in distributing their products.

# *Part* IV

## PRACTICAL USES OF THE HOBBY

# 11. "Good Work Makes Beautiful Things"

To complete the quotation from Lord Dunsany, let us add "and good work lasts." Furthermore, beautiful things are not created to be kept unseen and unknown. We all take pride in our own handiwork and we also enjoy admiring the work of others. So we try to make it possible for people to see our work and to develop their own skills and craftsmanship, and we also attempt to help those for whom a hobby is so necessary for its therapeutic values.

## Exhibits

There is a long way to go before pressed flower pictures and seed and citrus panels and plaques capture the imagination of those who manage exhibits. Largely because the art has been fairly limited up until now, proper exhibition in the shows to which they naturally are related have been few.

I have been lucky with my own work. From the time many years ago when the Garden Club of America borrowed a number of my pictures after they had been shown by the Horticultural Society of New York, they have been included in the Garden Club's exhibits at the New York International Flower Show almost yearly. The exhibits, it can be fairly said, do attract a good deal of audience interest and attention. Similar local and state organizations in other areas should be encouraged to make such exhibitions of well-done work possible.

It would seem reasonable that shows which exhibit table settings, fresh and dried flower arrangements, and various other horticultural displays would welcome a fresh addition to their list. The pressed flower hobbyist is going to have to become his own publicist and work for the inclusion of his hobby. Sometimes the one-man exhibit might be acceptable in conjunction with the regular exhibit, especially where there is no competition involved and of course no awards. Whenever the exhibit is competitive, the usual first, second, third honors should be given and possibly a special award can be arranged under the sponsorship of a club or an individual.

---

ILLUSTRATION 47

The seven daisies are the focal point of this arrangement, the bamboo forms the vertical line, the gingko leaves the lower solids, with mimosa the outer edges. Background: white rayon textured cloth; frame: white.

## PRACTICAL USES OF THE HOBBY

So many different types of work can be made with pressed flowers, as you have seen in this book, so it should not be difficult to set up a schedule of categories that will attract the attention of show managers. If you live in an area where the crafts are popular, there are always state and county fairs, craft fairs, and other local organizations which can be sounded out. It's your hobby and you must do the job of selling it.

### A Craft from a Hobby

Dictionaries vary on the first meaning of craft. But craft of which I speak is the one that emphasizes "skill and ingenuity in any calling, especially in a manual employment; hence, an occupation or employment, a trade." Except for the last word this is a pretty good definition of a hobby. Certainly skill and ingenuity, certainly the use of the hands are components.

Whether you give the products of your hobby away as gifts or sell them is of little importance except in one

---

ILLUSTRATION 48

A memory picture. The fern and the four, five, six, and seven petaled clover leaves were taken from the scrapbook of the author's grandmother. Only the fern and one petal failed to hold its color after eighty years. Background: textured maroon construction paper; frame: walnut.

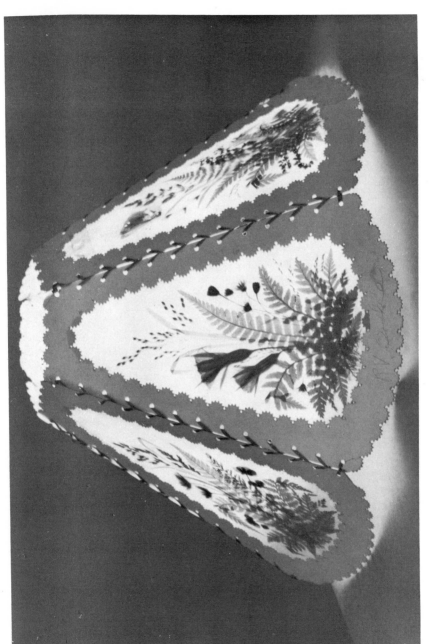

ILLUSTRATION 49

This lampshade is well over one hundred years old and came from Denmark to America by way of St. Thomas, when the island was in the Danish West Indies, that is, before 1917. There is no indication that adhesive was used to hold the pieces in place, although albumen may have been thing. That one thing is the value you put on your time if you sell your production. Therefore it is necessary to reserve your time for your true hobby for pleasure on the one hand and concentrate on the production of items that you can profitably sell for the other. You may, for example, make many things for church fairs or charity bazaars where you contribute your labor and materials. But for pin money or income from an occupation, you should concentrate on what you do quickly and well, objects for which there is a market, public or private.

Young and old and those in-between can learn to use pressed flower, seed, and citrus-fruit materials for the production of salable items. But don't undertake this craft without considering the time you have available, the cost of equipment and supplies (which is relatively small), and the working space you have at your disposal—all hobbyists find this last a problem, together with the need for an understanding family group.

Aside from the pressed flower pictures, there are paperweights, Christmas cards, tallycards, decorated matchboxes, bookmarks, blueprints, inkprints, spatter prints, miniatures, pins, small mosaics, citrus-fruit decorations, greeting cards for special occasions, party favors, gift-box decorations, pintrays and other small trays under glass, and as many more items as your imagination and ingenu-

185

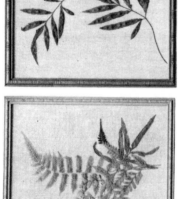

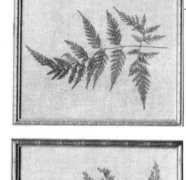

ILLUSTRATION 50

Fern prints. The specimens are arranged to show both top and undersurface of the leaf. Top: left, several greenhouse ferns; right, *Davillia pentaphylla*. Bottom; from the left, *Tectaria trifoliata*, *Selaginella cuspidata* var. *Emiliana*, *Davillia dissecta*, *Dryopteris dentata*.

ity can devise. For special-order work always be sure you have taken into account the cost of materials, your time, and profit.

A factor of importance in doing craft work such as this is that you make a number of similar items at one time. In this way you save time in assembling both the working materials and the finished work. You also give your customer a wider choice for selection, for remember that not everyone will like the same design or pattern for a particular piece. It is also possible to keep your prices within reason this way, for you buy supplies at lowest possible quantity prices.

## A Hobby and Its Therapeutic Value

A hobby is often an antidote for the strains and worries we all undergo at one time or another and for those who have too much time on their hands. The hobby that is the subject of this book is very good therapy for the man or woman or teen-ager who has an interest in flowers and plantlife and access to it and who realizes that worrying solves no problems. He is his own physician.

But there are more unfortunate people who cannot simply take up a hobby, but to whom the hobby must be brought. This group may include those who need rehabilitation after illness or accident. There are those whose physical handicap has fortunately left the hands and eyes reasonably functional; there are the elderly with lagging time to be occupied, or the chronically ill for whom most activity is proscribed. People such as these often find real release if this hobby is brought to them.

# 12. Lists for Guidance

*Some Flowers and Foliages for Pressing*

Variant names are given where possible and the classification is first by common name, since so many in this list are hardly known otherwise. Colors of available flowers may be supplemented in many areas. Character of drying quality is indicated broadly. Approximate drying time is stated, but atmospheric conditions strongly affect it. Almost all of the plants given here have been used in the illustration of this book.

ACACIA (Wattle). *Acacia pubescens*—Excellent. Press in small pieces; also yellow blossoms separately. About seven days.

AGERATUM (Floss flower or mist-flower). *Eupatorium coelestinum*—Excellent. Blue, lavender, white. Press in small pieces. About five days.

ALBIZZIA (Mimosa; silk-tree). *Albizzia julibrissi*—Excellent. Pink, lilac. Press flowers and leaves separately. About seven days.

PRACTICAL USES OF THE HOBBY

ALKANET (African forget-me-not). *Anchusa myosotidiflora* —Good. True blue. About seven days.

ALYSSUM (Sweet alyssum). *Alyssum maritimum*—Excellent. Garden hybrids, white, pink, lavender, purple, rose. About five days.

ALYSSUM (Golden-tuft, basket-of-gold, carpet-of-gold). *Alyssum saxatile compactum*—Excellent. Press in small pieces. About five days.

ANEMONE (Windflower). *Anemone coronaria*—Excellent. Garden hybrids, white, lavender, purple, red. Press flowers and leaves separately. About ten days. Many wild varieties.

APPLE BLOSSOMS. *Malus*—Poor. Pinkish white. Press flowers separately. Edges tend to turn brown. About five days.

ARCTOTIS (African-daisy, blue-eyed daisy). *Arctotis*—Garden hybrids, white, brown, yellow, pink, red, mauve. Press flowers, stem and foliage separately. About seven days.

ASTER (Starwort, Michaelmas daisy). *Aster*—Good. Hardy. Blue, pink violet, white. Press flowers separately or as spray. Seven to ten days. Many wild types.

ASTER (China aster). *Callistephus chinensis*—Good. Annual. Garden hybrids, red, pink, white, blue, purple.

190

Press flowers separately, single, semidouble best. About five to seven days.

ASTER (Golden aster, golden star). *Chrysopsis marina*—Good. Seven to ten days.

AZALEA. *Azaleas*—Poor. Many varieties and colors, horticultural and native. Press flowers and leaves separately. Colors variable to hold. About five to seven days.

BABY'S BREATH. *Gypsophila elegans* or *paniculata*—Excellent. White, pink. Press separately or as spray. About three days.

BACHELORS-BUTTON (See Cornflower).

BEE BALM (Oswego-tea, bergamot). *Monarda didyma*—Good. Pink, red, purple-red. Press flowers and florets separately. About five to seven days.

BLACKBERRY BLOSSOMS. *Rubus*—White. Press flowers separately. About five days.

BLACK-EYED SUSAN and BROWN-EYED SUSAN (Coneflower). *Rudbeckia hirta* and *R. triloba*—Excellent. Yellow-orange. About seven days.

BLEEDING HEART (Fringed or plumy bleeding-heart). *Dicentra spectabilis* or *D. eximia*—Variable. Pinkish-red, purple-red. About fourteen days.

191

## PRACTICAL USES OF THE HOBBY

BLUE LACE FLOWER. *Trachymene* or *Didiscus caerulea*—
Excellent. Light blue. About five days.

BROWALLIA (Amethyst-flower). *Browallia elata*—Good.
Blue, violet, white. About five days.

BUGLE. *Ajuga reptans*—Excellent. Garden hybrids, pur-
plish-blue. About seven days.

BUTTER-AND-EGGS (Toadflax). *Linaria vulgaris*—Good.
Yellow and orange. About seven days.

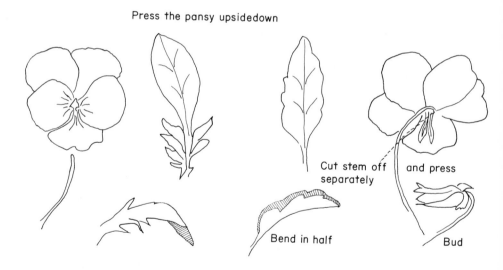

Fig. 11   Pressing the pansy

192

BUTTERCUP (Crowfoot, creeping buttercup). *Ranunculus repens*—Excellent. Yellow, single or double. About five days.

BUTTERFLY-BUSH (Buddleia). *Buddleja*—Poor. Garden hybrids, white, red, blue, pink. Tends to turn brown. About five days.

CALENDULA (Pot-marigold). *Calendula officinalis*—Excellent. Cream, yellow, orange. Holds color well. About ten days.

CALLIOPSIS. *Coreopsis tinctoria*—Excellent. Yellow, brown, maroon, variegated. About five days.

Put blossoms together
to form a flower

Separate blossom

You may press
something
like this

Fig. 12  Pressing the geranium

193

CANDYTUFT. *Iberis umbellata*—Excellent. Annual. Red, lilac, pink, blue, violet, white, colors muted. About five days.

CELOSIA (Ostrich-plume, cockscomb). *Celosia cristata* (crested) and *C. plumosa* (plumed)—Excellent. Yellow, pink, orange, red, white. Press in small pieces. About seven days.

CENTAUREA (Sweet sultan, knapweed). *Centaurea moschata* and *C. nigra*—Fair. Yellow, purple, white, and rose-purple. Press flowers separately. About ten days.

CHERRY BLOSSOMS. *Prunus*—Fair. Pink, white. Tend to turn brown. About five days. Many varieties.

CHICORY (Blue sailors, blue chicory). *Cichorium intybus* —Fair. Blue flowers sometimes dry pink. Press at once after picking. About five days.

CHINESE FORGET-ME-NOT. *Cynoglossum*—Blue. Good. About seven days.

CHRYSANTHEMUM. *Chrysanthemum*—Many types. Singles, excellent. Semidoubles, good. Various colors, yellow dries best. Press flowers separately and petals of very large flowers. About seven to fifteen days, variable.

CINQUEFOIL (Five-fingers) *Potentilla*. Many varieties. Excellent. Yellow commonest color. Very fragile. About five days.

CLEMATIS. *Clematis jackmani*—Good. Purple. Press flowers separately. About ten days to dry.

CLEMATIS (Virgin's bower, sweet autumn clematis). *Clematis virginiana* and *C. paniculata*. Good. White. About seven days.

CLEOME (Spider-flower). *Cleome spinosa*—Excellent. White, pink, salmon. Press flowers separately with plenty of foliage. About five days.

CLOVER (Common red clover, trefoil). *Trifolium pratense* —Excellent. About seven days. (Rabbit-foot clover). *T. arvense*—Blue-gray. Excellent. About seven days.

COLUMBINE. *Aquilegia*—Excellent. Many colors. Press flowers and foliage separately. About five to seven days.

CORAL BELLS (Alum-root). *Heuchera sanguinea*—Excellent. Yellow, pink, red, white. About seven days.

COREOPSIS (Tickseed). *Coreopsis lanceolata*—Excellent. Yellow, single or double. About five to seven days.

CORNFLOWER (Ragged-sailor, ragged-robin, bachelors-button, blue-bottle). *Centaurea cyanus*—Excellent. Blue, violet, pink, white, rose. About seven days.

195

COSMOS. *Cosmos bipinnatus,* and *C. sulphureus*—Excellent. White, crimson, pink, and yellow, orange. About seven days.

CROCUS. *Crocus vernus* and *C. aureus*—Fair. Purple, white, yellow. Tissue-like texture. Somewhat difficult. About five days.

CYPRESS-VINE (Red morning-glory). *Quamoclit pennata* and *coccinea*—Fair. Crimson. Somewhat difficult. About five days.

DAFFODIL (Jonquil). *Narcissus Pseudo-Narcissus*—Good. Yellow. About seven days.

DAHLIA. *Dahlia*—Many types and colors. Single hybrids best. All difficult. Often turn brown. About fourteen days.

DAISY (Field daisy, oxeye daisy). *Chrysanthemum leucanthemum*—Excellent. About five days.

DELPHINIUM (Larkspur). *Delphinium*—Annual and perennial types. Excellent. Blue, purple, white, pink. Press flowers separately and in spikes. About five days.

DOGWOOD (Flowering dogwood, cornel). *Cornus florida*—Poor. Pink, white. Tends to turn brown. About seven days. *On conservation lists.*

FERNS. Most ferns dry well in about seven days.

FEVERFEW. *Chrysanthemum parthenium*—Excellent. White, single and double. About seven days.

FLEECE-VINE (Silver lace-vine). *Polygonum auberti*—Good. White. About five days.

FORGET-ME-NOT. *Myosotis palustris semperflorens*—Blue. *M. palustris*—Blue, pink, white. Both good. About seven days.

FORSYTHIA (Golden-bells). *Forsythia suspensa*—Excellent. Yellow. About five days.

FOUR-O'CLOCK (Marvel-of-Peru). *Mirabilis jalapa*—Fair. Red, yellow, white. About five days.

FOXGLOVE. *Digitalis*—Fair. White, purple. Difficult to hold color. About seven days.

FUCHSIA. *Fuchsia*—Fair. Pink, white, purple, scarlet. Does not always hold color. About ten days.

GAILLARDIA (Blanket-flower). *Gaillardia*—Excellent. Orange, yellow, red. About five days.

GERANIUM (Cranesbill). *Pelargonium*—Many types. Excellent. White, pinks, reds. True colors. About five to seven days.

197

GEUM. (Avens). *Geum*—Many species. Good. Yellow, orange. About five days.

GLADIOLUS. *Gladiolus*—Good. Various colors, pinks, yellows best. Press only the blossoms. About ten days.

GLOBE AMARANTH. *Gomphrena globosa*—An everlasting. Excellent. White, pink, rose. About seven days.

GOLDENGLOW. *Rudbeckia laciniata*—Excellent. Yellow. Press flowers separately. About five days.

GOLDENROD. *Solidago*—Many species and varieties. Excellent. Press small pieces. About five to six days.

GRAPE HYACINTH. *Muscari botryoides*—Excellent. Blue, white, flesh (rare). Discard foliage. About seven days to dry.

HAWTHORN (Red haw, thorn). *Crataegus*—Many species and varieties. Good. English hawthorn, pink. Press flowers separately. About seven days.

HEATHER (Scotch heather). *Calluna vulgaris*—Excellent. Pink, white (rare). Press florets or spikes. About five days.

HEDGE MUSTARD. *Sisymbrium officinale*—Good. Yellow. About five days.

198

HELIOTROPE (Turnsole). *Heliotropium*—Good. White, violet. Press in small pieces or spray. About five days.

HEMEROCALLIS (Daylily). *Hemerocallis*—Fair. Tissue-like texture. Many varieties and colors, orange, yellow, red, pink, cream. About fourteen days.

HOLLYHOCK. *Althaea rosea*—Fair. White, yellow, pink, red. Tissue-like texture. Handle carefully. About five days.

HONESTY (Money-plant, St. Peter's-penny, satin-pod, satin-flower). *Lunaria annua*—Excellent. Press flowers, leaves, and seed disk separately. About five days.

HONEYSUCKLE (Common honeysuckle). *Lonicera japonica* —Fair. Sometimes browns. About five days.

HYDRANGEA. *Hydrangea*—Excellent. Pink, blue, lavender. Press florets and some petals separately. Colors will change variably. About five days.

JOE-PYE-WEED. *Eupatorium purpureum*—Good. Purple, lilac-pink. Press in sections, leaves separate. About five days.

JOINTWEED (Coast jointweed, sand heath). *Polygonella articulata*—Good. Rose, white, dark purple, dark red. About five days. Miscalled heather in New England.

199

# PRACTICAL USES OF THE HOBBY

LANTANA. *Lantana camara*—Good. Yellow, orange, pink, rose, white. About five days.

LARKSPUR (See Delphinium).

LAVENDER. *Lavandula vera*—Excellent. About five days.

LIATRIS (Blazing star, gay-feather). *Liatris scariosa*—Excellent. White, rose-purple. About seven to nine days.

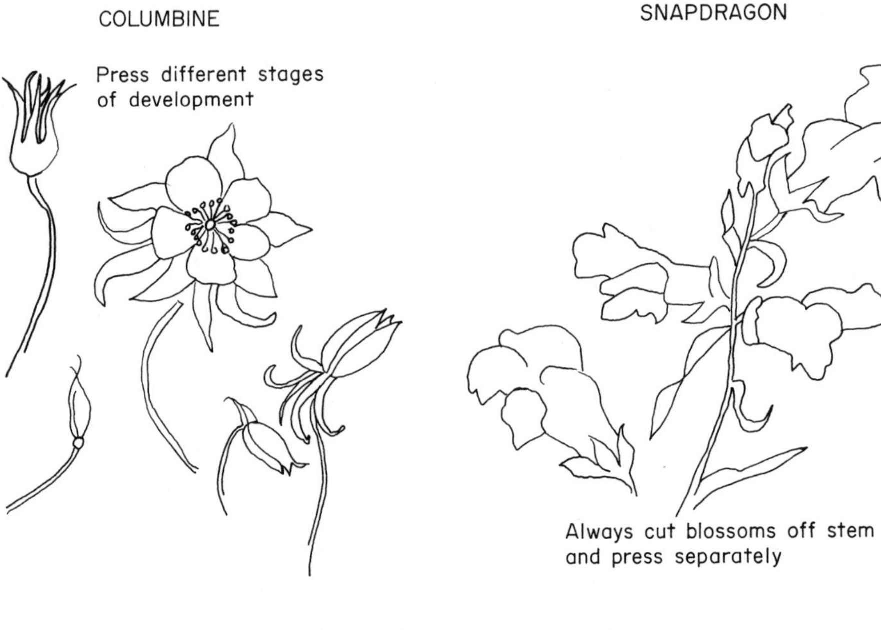

COLUMBINE

Press different stages of development

SNAPDRAGON

Always cut blossoms off stem and press separately

Fig. 13   Pressing the columbine and snapdragon

LILAC. *Syringa vulgaris* and *S. persica*—Poor. Rarely keeps color. Tends to turn brown. About seven to ten days.

LILY-OF-THE-VALLEY. *Convallaria majalis*—Very poor. Flowers and leaves turn tan or brown. About five days.

LOOSESTRIFE. (Spiked or purple loosestrife). *Lythrum salicaria*—Good. Magenta, purple. Press in three- or four-inch spikes. About seven days.

MARIGOLD. *Tagetes*—Excellent. Many types. Yellow, orange, mahogany, red and variegated. About ten days for singles; about fourteen days for double forms.

MIGNONETTE. *Reseda odorata*—Good. White and purple. About five days.

MILKWEED (Common milkweed, silkweed). *Asclepias syriaca*—Good. Pink. Press flower separately. Pod: open and press when light green; no leaves. About seven days.

MOCK-ORANGE (Syringa). *Philadelphus*—Good. Cream, white. Press flowers separately or as spray. About five days.

MORNING GLORY. *Ipomoea*—Good. White, red, blue, pink, purple. Tissue-like texture. About five to seven days.

MULLEIN (Verbascum, flannel-plant). *Verbascum thapsus*

201

—Excellent. Yellow. Press flowers separately and small leaves. About seven days.

NARCISSUS. *Narcissus*—Good. Many varieties. Yellow, white, cream, pink with pink, red, orange. About seven days.

NASTURTIUM. *Tropaeolum*—Fair. Many colors, single and double. Tissue-like texture. Difficult, but possible. Leaves turn yellow. About five days.

NICOTIANA (Ornamental or flowering tobacco). *Nicotiana affinis*—Fair. White, pink. Press flower only. Sometimes browns. About seven days.

NIGELLA (Love-in-a-mist, fennel-flower). *Nigella damascena*—Good. Blue, white. About five days.

PAINTED DAISY. *Pyrethrum roseum*—Good. Pink, red. About five days.

PANSY (Heartsease, Johnny-jump-up, when small-flowered form). *Viola tricolor hortensis*—Excellent. Many varieties, many colors. About three days.

PASSION-FLOWER. *Passiflora princeps*—Good. Pink, purple, and white. Refrigerate several days before pressing. Press with face down. About twenty-one days.

202

PEARLY EVERLASTING (Moonshine, immortelle, life-ever-lasting). *Anaphalis margaritacea*—Good. White. About three days.

PETUNIA. *Petunia hybrida*—Good. Many varieties, many colors. Tissue-like texture. Simpler forms best. Handle carefully. About five days.

PHLOX (Blue phlox, summer phlox). *Phlox divaricata* and *P. decussata*—Fair. Many colors. Press florets, not leaves. Sometimes browns. About five days.

PINKS (Garden pinks, garden carnations). *Dianthus*—Many annual and perennial forms. Excellent. White, red, pink. Foliage sometimes yellows. About five days.

PLANTAINLILY (Lanceleaf plantainlily or funkia). *Hosta lancifolia*—Good. Lavender. About five days.

POINSETTIA. *Euphorbia pulcherrima*—Excellent. Red, white. About seven days.

POPPY. *Papaver*—Good. Many annual and perennial forms. White, red, salmon, pink, yellow. Tissue-like texture. Handle carefully. About five days.

PRIMROSE. (Evening-primrose). *Oenothera biennis*—Good. Yellow. Press flowers separately. About five days.

203

QUEEN ANNE'S LACE (Wild carrot). *Daucus carota*—Excellent. White or cream. About five days.

ROSE. *Rosa*—Single varieties. Excellent. Various colors. About seven days. Also, Polyantha varieties. Pink and red best. Not all will do equally well. Press buds and half-open flowers and leaves. About seven days.

ROSE CAMPION (Pink mullein). *Lychnis coronaria*—Fair. Press flowers separately and small leaves. About seven days.

ROSE-MALLOW (Marshmallow, sea-hollyhock, swamp rose). *Hibiscus*—Fair. Cream-white with red or purple base. Tissue-like texture. Handle carefully. About seven days.

ROSE-OF-SHARON (Shrub-althea). *Hibiscus syriacus*—Good. White, rose, purple. Tissue-like texture. Handle carefully. About seven days.

SAGE (Scarlet sage and blue sage). *Salvia splendens* and *S. azurea*—Excellent. Red, blue, lavender. About five to seven days.

SALPIGLOSSIS (Painted-tongue). *Salpiglossis*—Good. Varicolored. About seven days.

SANVITALIA (Creeping zinnia). *Sanvitalia procumbens*—Excellent. Yellow, orange. About five days.

SCOTCH BROOM. *Cytisus scoparius*—Good. Yellow. Press four- or five-inch pieces when in bloom. About seven to ten days.

SEA LAVENDER (Statice, marsh rosemary. *Limonium carolinianum*—Excellent. Lavender-pink. About five days.

SHASTA DAISY. *Chrysanthemum maximum*—Excellent. White, yellow. About five days for singles; seven days for double varieties.

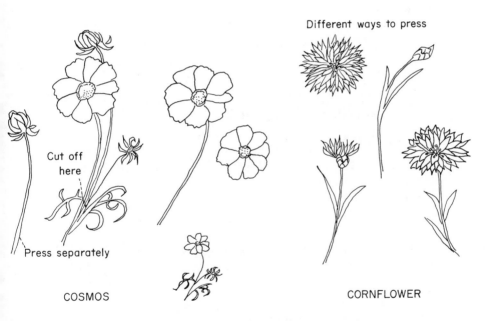

Fig. 14  Pressing the cosmos and cornflower

SIBERIAN SQUILL (Wild or wood-hyacinth). *Scilla sibirica*—Excellent. White, lavender, blue, pink. About five days.

SNAKEROOT (White snakeroot). *Eupatorium rugosum*—Good. White. About five days.

SNAPDRAGON. *Antirrhinum*—Good. Pink, yellow, white best. Press flowers separately. About seven to ten days.

SNOWDROP. *Galanthus nivalis*—Good. White. About five days.

SNOWFLAKE. *Leucojum vernum*—Good. White. Do not press leaves. About five days.

SNOW-ON-THE-MOUNTAIN. *Euphorbia marginata*—Excellent. Press principally for the leaves. About five days.

SPIDERWORT. *Tradescantia virginiana*—Good. Press only the blue flowers. Tissue-like texture. About five days.

SPIREA (Astilbe, false goatsbeard). *Astilbe japonica*—Excellent. Cream, pink, red. About five to seven days.

STAR-OF-BETHLEHEM (Nap-at-noon). *Ornithogalum umbellatum*—Excellent. White with green. About five to seven days.

STATICE (Sea lavender). *Limonium latifolium*—Lavender,

pink. *L. sinuatum*—rose, white, blue, yellow, violet, both excellent. About five days.

STOCK (Gilliflower). *Matthiola incana*—Excellent. White, red, pink, blue, purple. About seven days.

SUNFLOWER. *Helianthus*—Many species. Excellent. Small-flowered varieties best. About seven to ten days.

SWEET PEA. *Lathyrus odoratus*—Very poor. Difficult, seldom holds color. About five days.

SWEET WILLIAM. *Dianthus barbatus*—Good. White, pink, reds variegated. Press separate flowers or in small clusters. About seven days.

TANSY (Common tansy, golden-buttons). *Tanacetum vulgare*—Excellent. Yellow. About five days.

TASSEL-FLOWER (Devils-paintbrush, orange hawkweed, Canada hawkweed). *Brickellia* and *Emilia*—Good. Yellow, orange. About seven days.

THIMBLEFLOWER. *Gilia capitata*—Excellent. Blue-violet. About five days.

THUNBERGIA (Clock-vine). *Thunbergia*. (Black-eyed Susan vine). *Thunbergia alata*—Good. Orange to white, dark eye. About seven days.

207

TRUMPET-VINE (Trumpet-creeper). *Campsis radicans*—Fair. Orange-scarlet. Press flowers separately. About ten days.

VERBENA. *Verbena*—Excellent. Multi-colored annuals and perennials. Press flowers and leaves separately, or in small clusters. About five days.

VERONICA (Speedwell). *Veronica*—Good. Many types. Blue. About ten days.

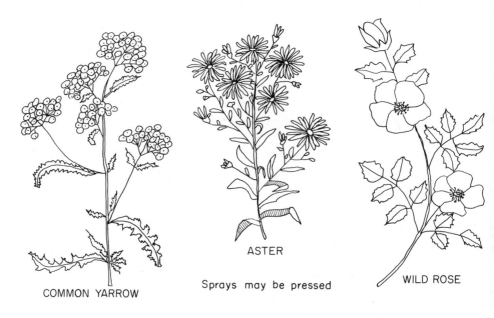

COMMON YARROW

ASTER

Sprays may be pressed

WILD ROSE

Fig. 15   Sprays—arrangement for pressing

VERVAIN (Blue verbena). *Verbena hastata*—Good. Blue. About seven days.

VIOLET. *Viola*—Many species and varieties. Very poor. Turns cream color. Leaves do not always hold color. About five days.

WILD INDIGO (Rattleweed, false indigo). *Baptisia australis* and *B. tinctoria*—Good. Blue, yellow. Leaves dry black. About seven days.

WILD SWEET PEA (Goat's rue, catgut, rabbit's pea). *Tephrosia virginiana*—Fair. Yellowish-white with purple. About seven days.

WISTERIA (Chinese). *Wisteria sinensis* and (Japanese) *W. floribunda*—Poor. White, blue. Rarely holds color and browns. About five days.

YARROW (Milfoil, achillea). *Achillea millefolium*—Good. White. About seven days.

ZINNIA (Youth-and-old-age, cut-and-come-again). *Zinnia*—Excellent. Most varieties and colors usable. Press flowers of larger varieties separately. About five days for singles, seven days for doubles.

PRACTICAL USES OF THE HOBBY

*More Foliage*

In pressing foliage, besides that which is useful from flowers, plants, grasses, weeds and so forth, be sure to have some on hand that provides the glaucous shades, the sea-greens and bluish-grays. By including these shades, you deepen the other greens and accent the beauty of light-colored flowers. Among those most easily to be had in your own or nearby gardens are lavender cotton, southern-wood, and members of the mullein and sage families. The artemesias, such as silver king, silver mound, and the dusty millers, are especially good also for their interesting leaf shapes.

Some popular unpopular weeds for pressing include the familiar

| | |
|---|---|
| buckhorn | purslane |
| dandelion | sheep sorrel |
| ground ivy | shepherd's purse |
| knotweed | speedwell |
| mallow | spurge |
| plantain | yellow trefoil |

Among the many grasses and grains which can be used to soften the outlines of many a design, or for botany prints, are

210

| | |
|---|---|
| barley | oats |
| beard grass | pampas grass |
| bur grass | quack grass |
| crab grass | timothy |
| darnel grass | wheat |
| foxtail grass | witch grass |

Bamboo, so widely used in Oriental art and especially by the Japanese, is already grown in some areas of the country. A new variety that is hardy in northern states has recently become available. You will find bamboo a choice addition to many designs. This plant presses well and its colors hold true, and the variegated green foliage is most effective against plain, simple backgrounds when used alone. To the Oriental mind, bamboo is the symbol of family loyalty, long life, happiness, and endurance.

In addition to the material suggested above, the fall leaves must not be overlooked. The brilliant colors of tree leaves will most certainly suggest some special ways in which they can be used. If you live in an area in the United States to which this seasonable time of spectacular beauty does not come, perhaps you might arrange with a friend to press for you; New England, New York and neighboring states, the Great Smokies and Arizona in the Southwest have notable natural exhibits. The trees here

211

listed are only a few of those that welcome the fall with signal displays of color.

American hornbeam—bright orange
Aspen—sulphur yellow
Beech—yellows
Birch—yellow
Black oak—dull red to orange brown
Dogwood—brilliant crimson
Gingko—sunset gold
Mountain ash—purple
Pink oak—rusty red
Red maple—bright scarlet-orange
Red oak—dark red to russet
Sassafras—blood-orange
Scarlet oak—beautiful reds
Sugar maple—orange, scarlet, yellow
Sumac—bright red
Sweet gum—flaming crimson
White oak—deep red to orange
Willow—gray-green

*Florists' Flowers*

Mention has been made earlier of the fact that florists' flowers may be pressed. For bridal memory pictures, for example, they are often necessary. You can press these flowers, often quite successfully, if you leave them lying for a while on newsprint, so that the water has a chance to dry out from the stems. Remember that by capillary action moisture in the stem feeds the blossoms for quite a while, and the florist has been keeping them fresh by immersing them in deep water containers for long periods. As much moisture as possible must be removed. You cannot expect the results to be as good as with freshly picked, unwatered flowers but this experiment may be well worth a try.

*State Flowers and Trees*

This list represents the flower and tree selected either by legislative action or by custom by the various states, as their symbol from the world of plant life. They are used whenever appropriate in the same manner as the state flags and seals.

| STATE | FLOWER | TREE |
|---|---|---|
| Alabama | camellia | longleaf pine |
| Alaska | forget-me-not | — |
| Arizona | saguaro | blue paloverde |
| Arkansas | apple blossom | shortleaf pine |
| California | California poppy | California redwood |
| Colorado | Colorado columbine | blue spruce |

PRACTICAL USES OF THE HOBBY

| STATE | FLOWER | TREE |
|---|---|---|
| Connecticut | mountain laurel | white oak |
| Delaware | peach blossom | American holly |
| District of Columbia | American Beauty rose | scarlet oak |
| Florida | orange blossom | cabbage palmetto |
| Georgia | Cherokee rose | live oak |
| Hawaii | red hibiscus | coconut |
| Idaho | syringa (Lewis mock orange) | western white pine |
| Illinois | butterfly violet | bur oak |
| Indiana | peony | tuliptree (yellow-poplar) |
| Iowa | wild prairie rose | — |
| Kansas | sunflower | eastern cottonwood |
| Kentucky | goldenrod | tuliptree (yellow-poplar) |
| Louisiana | southern magnolia blossom | — |
| Maine | eastern white pine cone and tassel | eastern white pine |
| Maryland | black-eyed Susan | white oak |
| Massachusetts | trailing arbutus | American elm |
| Michigan | apple blossom | white pine |
| Minnesota | showy ladyslipper | red pine |

| STATE | FLOWER | TREE |
|---|---|---|
| Mississippi | southern magnolia blossom | southern magnolia |
| Missouri | hawthorn | flowering dogwood |
| Montana | bitterroot lewisia | ponderosa pine |
| Nebraska | giant goldenrod | American elm |
| Nevada | big sagebrush | singleleaf pinyon |
| New Hampshire | purple lilac | paper birch (white birch) |
| New Jersey | butterfly violet | northern red oak |
| New Mexico | soaptree yucca | pinyon (nut pine) |
| New York | rose | sugar maple |
| North Carolina | flowering dogwood | — |
| North Dakota | wild prairie rose | American elm |
| Ohio | scarlet carnation | Ohio buckeye |
| Oklahoma | Christmas American mistletoe | eastern redbud |
| Oregon | Oregon grape | Douglas fir |
| Pennsylvania | mountain laurel | eastern hemlock |
| Rhode Island | violet | red maple |
| South Carolina | Carolina jessamine | cabbage palmetto |
| South Dakota | American pasqueflower | black hills spruce |
| Tennessee | iris | tuliptree (yellow poplar) |

| STATE | FLOWER | TREE |
|---|---|---|
| Texas | bluebonnet (Texas lupine) | pecan |
| Utah | sego lily | blue spruce |
| Vermont | red clover | sugar maple |
| Virginia | flowering dogwood | — |
| Washington | coast rhododendron | western hemlock |
| West Virginia | rosebay rhododendron | sugar maple |
| Wisconsin | butterfly violet | sugar maple |
| Wyoming | Wyoming paintedcup (paintbrush) | balsam poplar (cottonwood) |

## Conservation

Every garden club member, every visitor to state and national parks becomes aware that conservation of wildlife, both plant and animal, and of other natural resources, such as water supply should be his concern. Sometimes the action taken to protect wildlife is by law of the state or local community. Sometimes it is voluntary, by a group or organization. The lists that follow indicate the way conservation is being handled in my area and state. It would be a good idea for you to ascertain what your area does before you unwittingly violate the rules.

The State of New York prohibits the picking or uprooting of the following plants statewide: all native ferns;

216

lotus, *Nelumbium luteum;* mountain-laurel, *Kalmia lati-folia;* trailing-arbutus, *Epigaea repens;* fringed gentian, *Gentiana crinita;* closed gentian, *Gentiana clausa;* flowering dogwood, *Cornus florida;* lady's-slipper, all native *Cypripedium.*

In the Long Island district of the Federated Garden Clubs of New York State, the following plants may not be used or displayed in flower shows: American holly, *Ilex opaca;* bellwort, *Uvularia sessilifolia;* bloodroot, *Sanguinaria canadensis;* dwarf ginseng, *Panax trifolium;* ground- or running-pine, *Lycopodium clavatum;* Indian pipe, *Monotorpa uniflora;* inkberry, *Ilex glabra;* Jack-in-the-pulpit, *Arisaema triphyllum;* partridge-berry, *Mitchella repens;* Trillium, all varieties; trout-lily, *Erythronium americanum;* wild rose, all varieties; winterberry, *Ilex verticillata.*

In one of my pictures I have used the sensitive fern but it was grown in my garden and has been there for many years. Seed for some of the prohibited plants may be obtained from seed specialists for growing in your own garden.

As different regions of the United States vary so widely in wild plant life, the protected plants will vary considerably from state to state. So know and protect your own wild flowers.

217

# Index

Figures printed in *italics* indicate that an illustration will be found at the page listed. Roman figures refer to Color Plates.

# INDEX

backgrounds, picture, backing for, 36
  fabric, method for, 35-36
  materials for, 33-35
  mounting of, 34
  paper, art work on, 34, 80
  for passe-partout, 118, 120
  petal-point, 61-*64*-66, *I*
  plant material for, 34
Bailey, Liberty Hyde, 95-97
balance in design, 42, 44, 48
balsam, 41
bamboo, *68, 70, 74, 88, 180,* 211
banana skins, 175
*Baptisia australis, tinctoria,* 209
batchelors-button, 191
bee balm, 191
bellwort, 217
bergamot, *92,* 191, *II, VI*
Berton Plastics, Inc., 122
blackberry blossom, 191
black-eyed Susan, 6, *72, 92,* 110, 191, *III*
bleeding heart, 191
bloodroot, 217
blue lace flower, 192
blueprints, *112,* 113-115
boneset, *I*
botany prints, *106*-110, 111
bouquets, bridal, *96, 97,* 98-*99*-100
  dried, copying of, 66-72
*Brickellia,* 207
broom, Scotch, 131, 205
Bromo Spray-it-yourself Plastic Preservative, 176
browallia *(B. alata),* 192, *II, III*
bugle, 193

*Buddleja,* 192
butter-and-eggs, 192
buttercup, *92, 109,* 110, 193
butterfly-bush, *112,* 193

caladium, 88
calendars, 74, *75,* 76
calendula *(C. officinalis), 46, 66,* 193, *III*
calliopsis, 193, *III*
*Calluna vulgaris,* 198
*Callistephus chinensis,* 190
*Campsis radicans,* 208
candytuft, 7, 194
cardboard for backing, 35
cards, decorated, 115, 117, 185
cedar, 3, *80,* 91
celosia *(C. cristata, plumosa),* 28, *64, 66,* 74, *76, 92, 112, 126, 144,* 194, *I, II, III, VI*
*Centaurea cyanus,* 195
centaurea *(C. moschata, nigra),* 194
cherry, 194, *III*
chicory, 194
Chinese forget-me-not, 194
China aster, 190
chrysanthemum *(Chrysanthemum) 31, 46, 92,* 194, *II, III*
  legend of, 123-*124*
*Chrysanthemum leucanthemum,* 196
  *maximum,* 205
  *parthenium,* 197
*Chrypsosis marina,* 191
*Chichorium intrybus,* 194
cinquefoil, 194

220

# INDEX

framing *(cont.)*
  plastic, 121
  of seed pictures, 162-163
  selection of, 28-32
  shadow box, 162-163
  trays made from, 71-72
freesia, *28, 31, 46, 92,* 93, 94
fruit. *See* banana, citrus skins,
  pepper, seed.
fuchsia *(Fuchsia),* 197
funkia, 203

gaillardia *(Gaillardia),* 197, *III*
*Galanthus novalis,* 206
Garden Club of America, 179
"Gardener's Heritage, The," 95-97
gentian, 217
*Gentiana, clausa, crinita,* 217
geranium, 7, *28,* 142, *144, 193,* 197,
  *III*
geum *(Geum),* 198
*Gilia capata,* 207
gingko, *180*
ginseng, 217
gladiolus *(Gladiolus), 28, 70,* 198,
  *V*
glue. *See* adhesive.
globe amaranth, 198, *III*
goldenglow, 198
*Gomphrena globoso,* 198
goldenrod, *24, 46, 66, 92,* 110, 198,
  *I, III, VI*
grains, *62,* 78, 211
grape hyacinth, 131, 198
grasses, 4, *26, 28, 62,* 78, 117, 211
ground-pine, 217

*Gypsophilia, elegans, paniculata,*
  191

handicraft, considered as, 160, 182-
  184
hawthorn, 198, *I, VIII*
heat, artificial, for fruit skins, 168,
  175
  in pressing, 12, 20
heather, 6, *31,* 78, *144,* 198
hedge mustard, 198
helenium, 6, *92, III*
*Helianthus,* 148, 207
heliotrope *(Heliotropium),* 199
Hemerocallis *(Hemerocallis),* 199
*Heuchera sanguinea,* 195
holly, American, 217
hollyhock, 6, 146, 199
honesty, 66, 199
  pod partitions of, 34
honeysuckle, 143, 199
Horticultural Society of New
  York, 91-94, *95*
hosta *(H. lancifolia), 28, 31, 144,*
  *VIII,* 203
hibiscus *(H. syriacus),* 204
hydrangea *(Hydrangea),* 7, *26,* 28,
  *31, 32, 64, 144,* 199, *III, VIII*

*Iberis umbellata,* 194
*Ilex, glabra, opaca, verticillata,*
  217
Indian pipe, 217
ink prints, 117
International Flower Show, 91,
  182

# INDEX

224

# INDEX

plastic spray, 154, 158, 160, 171, 174, 176
poinsettia, 203
polyanthus rose, 204, *VIII*
*Polygonella articulata,* 199
*Polygonum auberti,* 197
poppy, 6, 203
*Potentilla,* 194
pressing, arranging for, 10-11, *12, 15, 17, 23, 24, 192, 193, 200, 205, 208*
  botanist's method of, 11-14
  drying time in, 20-22
  home method of, 14-20
  pruning before, 10-11, *23, 24, 208*
primrose, evening, 203
proportion in design, 41
pruning and shaping, 10-11, *23, 24, 208*
*Prunus,* 194
*Pyrethrum roseum,* 202

*Quamoclit, coccinea, pennata,* 196
Queen Anne's lace, *64, 66,* 204, *III, VI*

radiation in design, 41, *45*
*Ranunculus fascicularis, 109*
  *repens,* 193, *VI*
*Reseda odorata,* 201
Rex-N-Glue, 121
rhythm in design, 41
*Rosa,* 204
rose, *68, 74, 92, 98, 118,* 143-*144,* 204, *V*
  wild, 217

rose campion, 204
rose-mallow, 204
rose-of-Sharon, *88,* 204
*Rubus,* 191
*Rudbeckia hirta,* 191
  *lacinita,* 198
  *triloba,* 191

sage, 204
salpiglossis *(Salpiglossis),* 204
salvia, *72, 144, III, VIII*
  *S. azurea, splendens,* 204
sampler, lettering for, 104, 105
  needlework, 101-103
  pressed flower, 104-105, *VI*
sand heath, *32, 74, 76*
*Sanguinaria canadensis,* 217
sanvitalia *(S. procumbens),* 204, *II, VI*
scilla *(S. sibirica), 31, 88,* 206, *VIII*
sea lavender, *24, 64, 66,* 78, 205, *III*
seed, 151-153, *155*
  for botany prints, *106,* 108
  with citrus skins, 172, *173*
  mosaics, 160-161
  murals, 161-162
  pressing, 6
  types of, 153-156
  using, 152-162
*Selaginella cuspidata,* 186
sepia arrangements, *8*
shadow box framing, 162-163
shasta daisy, 205
shellac, 176
  for citrus skins, 169
  for seed work, 160

226

# INDEX

# NOTES

# NOTES

# NOTES

# NOTES

# NOTES

# NOTES

# NOTES

NOTES